1/2025

WHITE
KNUCKLES
LOG

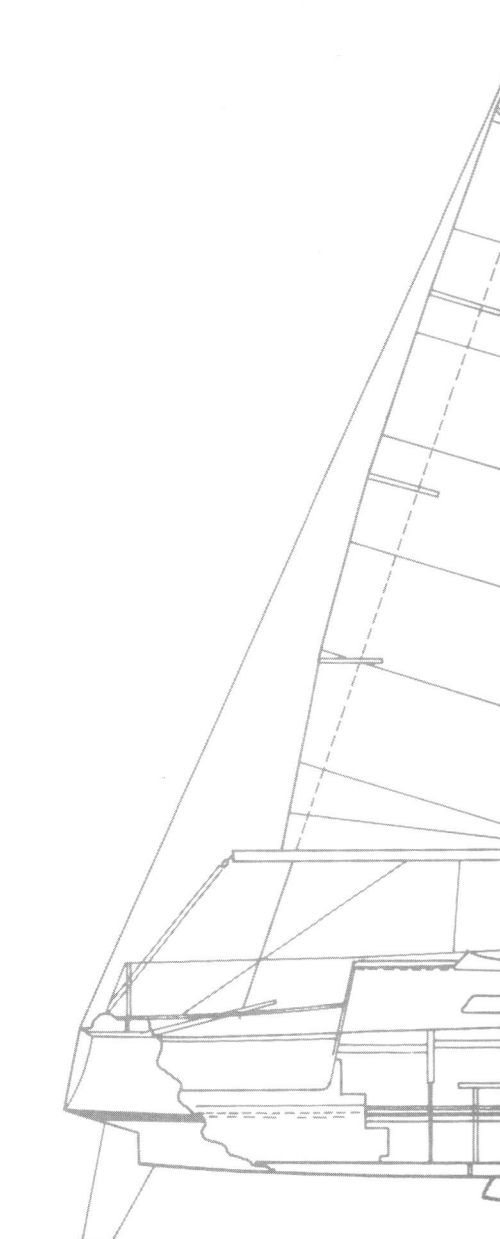

DON McALPINE'S
WHITE KNUCKLES LOG

EDITED BY MELBA McALPINE

Council Oak Books, Ltd., Tulsa, Oklahoma

Council Oak Books, Ltd.
1428 South St. Louis
Tulsa, Oklahoma 74120
© 1986 by Melba McAlpine
All rights reserved

Printed in the United States of America

Designed by Carol Haralson
Production management by Coman & Associates
Production by Karen Slankard
Illustrations by Carl Brune
Typography by Ann Weisman and Typo Photo Graphics
Maps courtesy of the U.S. Army Corps of Engineers

The maps are included for illustrative purposes only.
Do not use them for navigation.

LC 86-071127
ISBN 0-933031-05-X

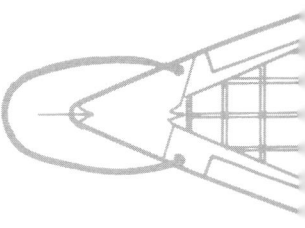

ACKNOWLEDGMENTS

I could not have fulfilled my dream without the help of some special people: Mr. Jim Jackson, Mr. Gerald Howard, Mr. Clarence Supple, my fine nephew Danny Worsham, and my son Willie. Some call my son "Sweet Willie," and if a father is allowed to be so sentimental, I wish to join Willie's following. I would also like to thank my good friend Don Van Meter and, especially, my wife Melba.

D. Mc A.

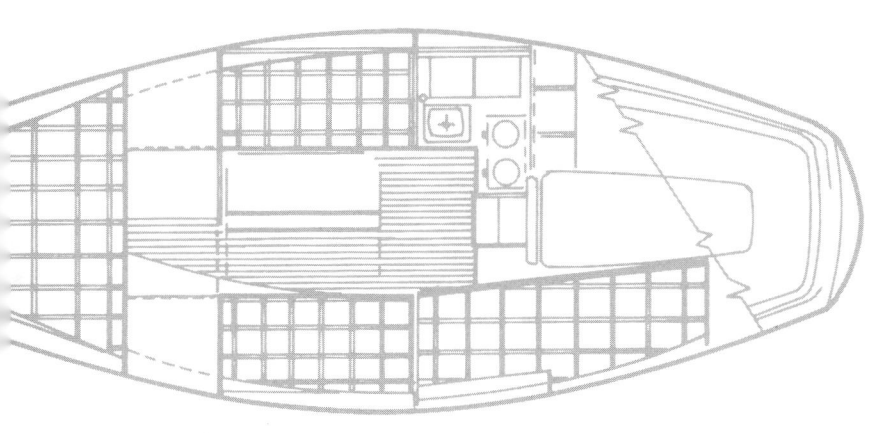

PROLOGUE

White Knuckles seeks the sea! *White Knuckles* — that's the name of the boat, the star of this saga. She's a twenty-five-foot, fiberglass sloop, built in 1977 by Hunter. I, Don McAlpine, am her tenant, her keeper, and, when I flatter myself, her skipper. She was given this name by her former owner, and I've never thought it proper to change a boat's name. So *White Knuckles* she will remain, although I sometimes take my prerogative to call her "*WK*" or just "Girl."

She is a gallant, kindly, and forgiving boat. She has, for example, already forgiven my many fumblings and bumblings in learning how to handle her. But she can be stubborn too. In the short time I have been on the river, I have had the experience of spying a likely looking creek in which to anchor for the night, only to have *White Knuckles* stick her fin deep into a mud bar, indicating that she would go no farther. She just didn't like that creek.

Knowing when I was beaten, I told her, "Okay, Girl," and backed gently out of there. Then we searched for another place to anchor that would please us both.

I had determined that *White Knuckles* and I would go from the head of navigation on the McClellan-Kerr Arkansas River Navigation System to the Gulf of Mexico and possibly beyond. I knew the boat was capable. Only time would tell if I was. Since I'd bought her, I'd kept the boat berthed at Oklahoma City's Lake Hefner, which is landlocked. That lake was the only place I'd sailed.

Now, in my defense, Lake Hefner can be treacherous enough. It has capricious winds, shallow water, and sudden storms — sometimes even tornadoes. In fact, a sailor friend once told me, "If you can safely sail Lake Hefner through one season, you can sail anywhere." I wanted to believe this, and I finally did — at least to the extent of deciding to attempt this journey from Catoosa, Oklahoma, to the Gulf of Mexico. Thus far, it has been a dream come true, a dream that first took shape in my mind over fifty years ago.

I was born and raised on a cotton farm in southwestern Oklahoma. I didn't like it. I have often felt I must have been born disliking the farm because I cannot remember a time when I did not desperately want to leave it. A small creek with the rather undignified name of Turkey Creek ran through our place. When I was very young, I asked someone where that creek went. I was told that it emptied into a fork of the Red River, which forms the border between Texas and Oklahoma. It didn't take much geographical study for me to find out that the Red River feeds into the Mississippi River, which leads to New Orleans and the ocean. With this discovery, my lifelong dream began.

In the beginning, it was only a boy's dream of building a boat, catching that little, insignificant Turkey Creek "on the rise," as we used to say, and floating away — away from the dry, dusty clime I had known and on to unknown shores and exotic places.

This dream of mine stayed alive (as dreams certainly should) in my heart and mind through my childhood and early manhood right on into my fifty-seventh year. The dream survived a world war with its lonely and desperate places in Africa, Sicily, Italy, France, and Germany. Coming home by ship after the war, I remember standing at the rail, looking out over the water, and thinking, "The water from Turkey Creek could be touching this ship right now." My dream has also survived three marriages, two divorces, the raising of a family, and retirement. Now it is time for that dream's fulfillment, before old age confines me to just dreaming again.

I've often wondered why I fixated on the sea when I was brought up so far away from *real* water. After all, it's a long way from Turkey Creek to the ocean. Perhaps one of my ancestors was a seafarer; but as far back as I can trace my Scotch-Irish-Dutch heritage, my people have always been of the land. However, I can look back to my childhood and remember that my elders seemed to be on a constant search for water; where I was raised, there was never enough of it. Can it be that my childhood lack of water later caused me to seek an abundance of it? It makes a nice theory.

Tonight, bone tired, wet, dirty, hungry, and cold, I think of the life I left behind in the city — the good, solid prairie that never gets too wet, the safe job in a strong, heated building — so secure as to be likened to a prison. How I long for it at times! Then comes a bright sparkling day aboard *WK* — and all thoughts of security leave my mind. I could not trade that slow drying and dying for this wetter and faster life. I feel that I belong on the bosom of the water, so that's where Girl and I are going.

Not that life on shore ever was a prison for me. The third time was the charm, in my case, when I married the kindest, most understanding woman on this earth. She didn't employ even one of the many arguments she could have to keep me from going on this journey. For that, I would like to nominate her as "Wife of the Century." I'm sure the shoe will be on the other foot someday, and I hope I can be half as understanding when she explains her dream to me.

Did I note that *White Knuckles* was built in Florida on the gulf? Perhaps that is the reason I feel that both of us are going home.

LOG

November 3

We're on the water!

In the early afternoon today, with the help of my youngest son, Willie, and my nephew Danny Worsham, *White Knuckles* was set into the Verdigris River near Inola, Oklahoma. It was a special moment indeed.

This morning we trailered *White Knuckles* from Oklahoma City — and that's no way to treat a boat. It was a beautiful day; "second summer" was in the air, a phenomenon not unusual at all in Oklahoma this time of year. The clear skies and warm temperatures seemed to bode well for the journey ahead, and I found my own spirits to be very high.

At the landing, we stepped the mast. Then we launched *White Knuckles*. She went into the water easily, and just as she floated off the trailer, a huge tow of barges appeared, rounding the bend and heading upriver. The river is quite narrow at this location, and that double row of barges seemed to fill all the available space. The wake of those boats could have tossed *White Knuckles* and me right back on the shore from which we had so recently come. But the captain must have noticed us because he slowed down — we were hardly tossed around at all. It was a nice gesture, and I couldn't help but think that the river is a friendly place. I offered up a silent prayer that it would remain that way.

My two good helpers said their good-byes at 1600, and I was left alone with my boat. I put in the time until dark storing supplies and trying to clear out enough room to give myself someplace to sleep. The initial chore was just getting everything outside the cabin inside; I finally managed to do so. Then I had my first meal alone on the water, dining sumptuously on cheese and crackers, which I washed down with coffee.

At the end of this first day, I feel good, perhaps better than I've ever felt. The anchor light is swinging in the rigging; the lamp in the cabin is glowing, providing enough warmth to keep me comfortable. I have the happy, lulling sensation that all is right with the world. I will sleep well tonight.

NOVEMBER 4
Mile 31.8, Verdigris River

The miles I give at the beginning of these entries come from the mileage markers along the river. They let me know how many miles I have to travel to the river's mouth.

On this, the second day, I was destined to make all of six miles. That was fine. I'd planned to spend the day sorting, storing, and cleaning anyhow. I also wanted to put in some time studying my charts and the *Rules of Inland Waterways*.

But I'm afraid I wasn't as productive as I might have been today. My good night's sleep didn't come to pass after all. Throughout the night, barges passed by my tiny sailboat.

I am astounded at how busy the waterway really is. The

barges, I must admit, scare the heck out of me. They're so big they seem to fill the whole channel. I don't look forward to meeting one while under way, although I know I will. I just hope it's in a straight part of the river.

And then there were some problems with the wind. It changed and increased a good deal, making my previous night's location unsafe. Otherwise, I might have opted not even to go the six miles.

But I've run down to Rocky Point, which has a nice cove, and I'm feeling quite safe for the night. Now to get some sleep!

NOVEMBER 5
Mile 27, Verdigris River
(Newt Graham Lock and Dam)

White Knuckles and I waited all morning for the weather to improve — it seemed that Oklahoma was living up to its reputation for bad weather at a moment's notice. But things got better, and we embarked in a cold, dead-ahead wind.

We arrived at our first lock. I'd prepared myself fully for this, and I followed procedure, sounding one long blast on *White Knuckles's* horn.

I got no answer.

I moved much closer, and sounded another blast. Still no answer. Was I doing something wrong?

The gates were closed, and I thought there might have been a boat entering from downstream. Deciding that retreat might be the best strategy, *White Knuckles* and I went to a nearby creek and waited. No boats passed in either direction.

I waited a bit longer, but it was getting late by this time. It seemed like a good idea to wait until morning. Perhaps then I could raft onto a barge to get through the lock. Having never negotiated a lock before, I had to admit to more than a little anxiety about it — and anxiety is something that always lessens in the clear light of day.

I'd had my share of other kinds of anxiety in the clear light of the day just passed, however. We'd come around some narrow, sharp bends in the river just hours before that had me literally sweating for fear of meeting a tow.

Anchoring has proven to be a consistent problem for me. I have no depth finder, and I must feel my way gently along for what I hope will be a good place to drop the hook. So far, each anchorage, for one reason or another, has necessitated the use of two anchors. They're hard to drop and hard to pull up. Tonight I moved from one uneasy anchorage to another, looking for a safe stop for the night. I'm not very happy with the location I finally chose. There's a strong current and a crosswind tonight, and if the wind increases, I'll have to seek another place.

So I am sleeping in my clothing tonight, and I'm setting the alarm for every hour. Yes, it's been a tiring day, and it may well be a tiring night. But the one thought I keep having, almost irrationally, is, "God, this is fun!"

November 6 and 7

For two days, I have been unable to travel any farther down the river. Yesterday, the wind was strong and just not right for anchoring at the arrival point for the lock. I motored over there, but I couldn't stay long enough to exchange the necessary signals for entrance. The weather has been cloudy and warm, but the wind is hampering our progress.

Today I got up early, determined to get through the lock. I got into position and gave one long blast, then dropped anchor and waited about an hour. Lo and behold, there was a long blast from the lock!

Did I get my hopes up at the very sound? I did. And did I move with great speed in the direction of the lock? I did. And all for nothing. There was a red light waiting for me. That long blast had been for a tow of barges heading upstream.

Then another tow passed. And then another. But I was not allowed to pass. So I sat out today, too. It wasn't a total loss; I visited with quite a few fishermen and, after a while, got to feeling like quite the old sailor.

A sailor who can't seem to get through the lock! Actually, I might have been able to get through at about 1700 hours, but I'd already moved out of position by then, tired and disappointed. I saw a green light come on, but I was simply too weary to see if it was for me. I hope I didn't make those fellows mad. I'd sure hate to wait out another day tomorrow.

November 8

I awoke this morning to cold, drizzling rain. It's hard to believe that yesterday was so warm, but that's Oklahoma. The rain, however, really got me going. I was determined from the beginning of the day that I was not going to spend another night there.

So I inflated the dinghy and rowed across the river. Then I walked the mile back to the lock and went down to have a talk with the lockmaster. If I couldn't maneuver this boat into the lock, I'd talk it in.

The lockmaster looked more like a cowboy than an old salt, but he also looked like he knew his business as he sized me up with a careful eye.

"Could you tell me if I'm doing something wrong?" I asked him. "I've been trying for two days to get my sailboat through."

The lockmaster laughed and offered me some coffee. "You know," he told me, "we just don't hear those little boats up here. We weren't snubbing you; we just didn't hear you."

I laughed, too, although he was feeling more amusement than I was. "Look," I told him, "I've got sixteen more locks to get through. Any advice?"

He refilled his cup, and offered the pot to me. "Next lock," he told me, "sail right up to the long wall, tie up there, and pull the signal chain that hangs from every one of them. Then just wait for clearance, and it won't take long."

"Thanks," I told him. "At the rate I was going, you just saved me several weeks."

"You still have to mind the big tows," he cautioned. "If one of those is coming through, it's best to skedaddle. The wake of those things will eat a boat like yours for breakfast."

I finished my coffee and asked the lockmaster if he would mind mailing some letters for me. He was happy to. He was also happy, as it turned out, to give me a guided tour of the lock. When I left, I felt a lot better. I'd been regarding that lock as a medieval fortress presided over by some wicked wizard with a warty nose. Instead, there was just a friendly Oklahoma cowboy lockmaster up there. I knew I was going to do much better with the next sixteen locks.

Back on *White Knuckles,* I tried to warm up but couldn't. The rain still fell, and I began to think about how ill-equipped I was, with so little waterproof or warm clothing. Buying some isn't going to be as easy as one might think. This waterway is like an interstate highway in that it doesn't go through towns. I've got a good shot at going shopping when I get to Muskogee, and that's about it for the next few days.

Then I looked around at some of my mail-order gadgets — the kind I'd ordered, as boat owners often do, because the pictures looked so nice. My fancy nautical articles hadn't come in all that handy, and I had a feeling that they'd wind up being consigned to the deep. Good thing they looked biodegradable.

Cold and wet as I was, I was on my way — at last!

November 9
Mile 3, Verdigris River

W*hite Knuckles* — if I had the booze, I'd be drinking a toast to you tonight. We've done something quite fine today. We've met our first tow of barges on the open water, and we have survived.

It was a formidable-looking tow, and it was making quite a few knots, heading straight for us. The captain gave two blasts on the horn, which I took to mean that he was going to pass off to starboard. That was fine with me. In fact, he could have passed anywhere he darned well pleased. That tow looked huge!

I steered as close to him as I dared in that narrow channel, trying to increase motor speed for better steerage. But his wake was awful. *White Knuckles,* you were tossed around like a cork, and I had to watch as your cabin quickly became a shambles. In fact, as I looked back at the huge tugboat pushing the barges, I was amazed that there seemed to be no water in the river immediately behind the tug. It was pushing so much water that it was — honestly — emptying the river.

I feel good about today, for more reasons than that my boat and I survived the tow. We're three miles from entering the Arkansas River, which has to be wider than the Verdigris. After all, I came on this trip to sail, and so far, it's been all motoring. The days ahead will surely allow for some sailing time.

I looked at myself in the cabin mirror tonight, and I've

started a good beard. *White Knuckles* isn't looking like a yacht-club boat herself anymore. There are anchors fore and aft, fenders port and starboard, an inflatable dinghy on the foredeck, and assorted gas cans, boat hooks, and an oar within reach. I also have an old canvas working jib with sheets and halyard attached; in case of a motor failure, I want to be able to get at least one sail up within seconds.

No, *White Knuckles,* you're not looking all that classy anymore. But you look ready, and that's what counts out here.

I'm learning another lesson in safety every night, by the way. The little creeks and inlets — even the river itself — have tides. The more the locks are used, the more the water level fluctuates, especially at short distances from the locks. Last night, for example, we anchored in an inlet that provided about eight feet of water. This morning, I found that *White Knuckles* was sitting on her keel, with the waterline stripe about six inches above the water.

As I was sitting there wondering what to do, an old fisherman strode up, seemingly out of nowhere. "Wait 'til the lock is used," he told me. "Just once. Then you'll be out of here."

He was right. Shortly thereafter, a large tow went upstream. I soon found that the water was rising. Before long, *White Knuckles* was floating free from her anchor.

November 10

At 0800 this morning, I experienced my first real tragedy of the trip, a death on board — the water pump. I was letting the motor warm up, hoping for a full day on the water, when I noticed it. I cursed my luck and dinked ashore, looking for a telephone from which to call a repairman.

I didn't find a telephone, but I did find two squirrel hunters who helped me get the motor off *White Knuckles* and onto the shore. Then they loaded it up and took us to an outboard-motor repair shop.

Along the way, the younger of the two turned to me and asked, "What kinda trip you on?"

"A long one, I hope," I told him. "This is my first serious stop."

"You do this all the time?"

"No," I said. "In fact, this is my first time. I'm a civil servant who decided to do something for myself for a change."

The older of the two laughed, a friendly sound.

"Got any family?" the younger one asked.

"I have a wife back in OKC," I told him. And I added, unnecessarily, "She didn't come."

The sky had clouded badly, and it was clear that a winter storm, maybe a big one, was on the way.

"Seems to me," the younger one said, "that I'd rather be home in a nice warm house."

"So why are you are out here squirrel hunting?" the

older hunter demanded. And we all burst out laughing.

The repairman figured three days on the motor, so I let the hunters take me back to *White Knuckles* to wait it out. I'll tell you the truth: I nearly set sail without the motor. But I looked at the weather, and I looked at the map. Approaching Muskogee, the channel went through a cut that looked extremely narrow. The chart specified a passing zone at either end of the cut, and that usually meant narrow. Not enough tacking room, I thought to myself, and I settled in.

A winter storm raged outside, but *White Knuckles's* cabin was surprisingly warm. By closing the door to the forward section, I found that I could stay warm all evening and all night with just one candle burning. On this first really cold night, my thoughts inevitably turned to home. I began to wonder why I had left my nice warm house, a comfortable inside job, and my fine loving wife. I thought that, even here, it wasn't too late to turn back.

But of course it is. I am braving this river for the same reason that mountain climbers climb the mountain — because it's there. In other words, I am staying with it. I am going the distance.

November 11

This was Veterans Day and easily the quietest Sunday I have ever spent. Lonesome, too. I walked into Okay, Oklahoma — what a name for a town! — and went shopping. I stocked up and, walking back, took in the change for the better in the weather. It was time to get moving again. The storm was over, and I was looking at a beautiful day.

I did some boat cleaning, wrote letters, and read. This should have been contentment, but it wasn't. Surely that motor would be ready tomorrow, I told myself.

November 12

The motor was ready. Late afternoon had arrived by the time I got the thing out of the shop, but we'll be away from here in the morning.

I dinked ashore three times today, loading up water, gasoline, more food, and the rebuilt motor. I walked about eight miles in the course of all this, too, and I feel physically excellent. I've gotten to know, over this two-day period, the very nice people of Okay. They all either envy me — or think I'm some kind of nut.

November 13
Mile 373, Arkansas River

A lot of people don't think there's much to look at in Oklahoma. A day like today would prove them wrong.

We didn't get to push off until after 1100. It took that long for the fog to lift. But when it did, a beautiful fall day was revealed, perfect for making the twenty-six miles that *White Knuckles* and I were able to log today.

And what country! We've been winding through hills that are golden and brown with the fall foliage. We dropped anchor tonight at Greenleaf Park, just upstream from Webbers Falls Lock. It's a beautiful spot, too, and the barometer is high. Things look good for tomorrow.

Things look good for hoisting sail, too, in about twenty miles. There will still be places where only that stinkpot of a motor will suffice on this river, and *White Knuckles* and I are both anxious to sail.

November 14
Mile 340, Arkansas River

This day gave us our best run so far. That doesn't mean it was satisfactory. We're still not sailing yet, and sailing days are the only really satisfactory ones for me. But aside from that, it was a good day.

Although Kerr Lake is large, it's very shallow and full of dead timber; one must stay in the buoyed channel. That, of course, was one reason for not sailing, but the main reason was the strong head winds that continue to plague us. There would have been too much tacking involved in sailing on a day like this.

The day was bright and sparkling, a real fall foliage tour. The water shimmered constantly, making it difficult to see very far, but the sun lit up the surrounding hills with color. Nature put on quite a show for us today.

There was one thing that marred the otherwise peaceful scene, however. Squirrel season is open, and all day long I got the feeling that a small war was raging on each bank. In truth, I was a little frightened of stray bullets — and you would have been, too. Most of the hunters were using shotguns instead of rifles, though, and shotguns don't carry as far.

Today, I couldn't help but wonder what a shotgun does to a squirrel. After such a blast, is there any meat left on those bones, anything left to eat at all? For that matter, do those hunters even eat their kill, or are they just killing squirrels? What if the squirrels had guns? It would seem much fairer than what I saw today.

Being on this river is making a rabid conservationist out of me. We're tied up tonight at a dock in Applegate Cove; it's the first night we haven't anchored. It's very peaceful here, and I feel quite at one with nature around me. Perhaps that's why my thoughts are wending toward such compassion for those squirrels.

Not having to anchor is a relief, though. Because of the currents, the crosswinds, and the ever-present bottom of silt, anchoring is a tremendous chore. It's not easy to hold this boat, especially when, during the night, a lock is opened upstream or one is closed downstream. The water level changes, and a different current is unleashed. In the morning, though, I'll just slip a couple of lines and be on my merry way.

NOVEMBER 15
Mile 302, Arkansas River
(Fort Smith, Arkansas)

Today the lack of wind kept me from sailing, but it was a wonderful day anyway, warm and bright. The section of river we passed through was very wide. I putted along at a slow speed, thoroughly enjoying the scenery. The current of the river has increased, because the Grand, Canadian, and Illinois rivers have all joined forces with the Arkansas. But it's still good water to go on.

My six-horsepower motor gets six miles to the gallon and goes six miles per hour. Three sixes — is that good luck? Or, as in the Bible, is it demoniac? I still think about my journey as a strange combination of light and dark forces working upon me, so maybe it's both.

We passed through the Robert S. Kerr and the W. L. Mayo locks today. Both signaled us right on in as we approached. I'm getting quite good at maneuvering these locks; it's always twice as windy around them, because the walls of the lock act as a funnel for the wind. Therefore, they must be approached slowly — under five miles per hour — with fenders port and starboard and mooring lines fore and aft. When I think we're approaching too fast, I ease the boat over against the wall and let the fenders act as brakes. And one line at the bow can serve both sides, provided it is long enough to reach back to the cockpit.

Tonight we're nestled in a quiet cove of Lee Creek. High bluffs and dense, rich foliage are all around *White Knuckles* and me. It's not as primitive as our other recent nights have been. I can hear the roar of traffic somewhere out there, and I can see the lights of Van Buren, Arkansas, over the lowest bluff. The rush of civilization is out there for me, very near if I wish to join it.

But I don't. Not tonight. On this night, the warm, glowing cabin and *White Knuckles* gently pulling at her bow anchor seem much more inviting. I'll read, think my long thoughts, and be happy.

November 16
*Mile 272, Arkansas River
(Ozark Lake, Arkansas)*

These days, as is common in this part of the country, are more like summer than the middle of November. Before noon today, I was down to my shirtsleeves. We only made about thirty miles, but I spent a good part of the morning in Van Buren taking on supplies. Once under way, we didn't stop until dark, and I had my lunch in the cockpit, as usual.

The river shows us a new scene around every bend. I feel that I'm watching a beautiful film that never ends. *White Knuckles* keeps pushing her bow curiously downstream, as eager as I am to see what lies ahead.

There has been a geographical change — we are about two hundred feet closer to sea level than when this adventure began. In about fifteen miles, we'll drop again as we enter Lake Dardanelle, Arkansas.

I looked up today and saw huge flocks of geese passing overhead.

"Well, *White Knuckles*," I said, "at least we have as much sense as geese. Everybody should be heading south at this time of year."

We may well beat Old Man Winter after all!

November 17
Mile 235, Arkansas River
(Lake Dardanelle)

I talked with several fishermen today. In the warm, spring-like weather, they were all out in their boats. Many came alongside, asking me where I was going.

"I'm just trying to see where the river will take me," I told a fellow about my age who was fishing with his son, who looked about sixteen.

"Where it'll take you?" he repeated. "Well, it'll take you to New Orleans."

"Then that's where I'm going," I replied. Both of them wished me well.

I'm seeing pine trees today for the first time. They blend in wonderfully with the color scheme of brown, gold, and red. In the distance now, I can see the foothills of the Ouachita Mountains, and they provide quite another color scheme. They are blue and hazy and seem so remote. Clearly, we're still a good distance from them.

The motor conked out again, just at dusk. I let the boat drift toward shore, thinking that it was just as well and that I could do without a motor. Of course I will need it; the locks present a real problem in that regard. Those fifty-two-foot-high walls create winds that are just too capricious for a sailboat.

I'm getting true sea legs — or river legs. I've commented on how I used to fear those meetings with barges and the tugboats that push those tows, but now I just shift the motor into neutral, turn *White Knuckles* toward shore, and coast. When the tow is even with us, I shift the motor to forward slow and turn my bow toward the wake of the barges. When the crest of the wake hits the boat, I increase motor speed and ease into the center of the wake, then I point the boat downstream. In that way, I make the wake work for me.

This seems trivial procedure, I know, but it's important to me. I'm learning to do things right on this river. But now the problem of the motor presents itself again, and I know I'll have to get it fixed, probably in Russellville. But that's for tomorrow.

Tonight, I've got to straighten up the shambles of my cabin. I didn't stow carefully enough last night, and the meeting with a tow I had today has made a fair mess out of things. There's nothing quite as irritating as coming below to a scrambled cabin after a hard day at the helm.

November 18 and 19
*Mile 206, Arkansas River
(Dardanelle Dam)*

I have just completed the longest stretch of two-day sailing — much longer than I ever did on those weekends at the lake — and I have thoroughly enjoyed it. Yes, I had Old Stinkpot repaired, but I also enjoyed being without that motor.

White Knuckles and I have been on Lake Dardanelle during this time. This lake is filled with innumerable islands, none of them very large. A few of these islands have gas wells on them, a depressing sign of progress in this otherwise sheltered area.

Signs of progress I've already mentioned — hunters — have been with us as well, and this time they're after ducks. Some of their boats were covered with tree boughs and cornstalks to fool the ducks, making strange-looking craft indeed. They didn't fool much of anything, though, because they spent most of their time blasting away with their guns.

Despite those hunters, yesterday's sailing was quiet and peaceful. *White Knuckles* seemed much more alive and responsive to me and would really shake herself out occasionally when a good wind got up. There was rain off and on. This morning I woke up to a dead calm.

That's where the fisherman I met found me, as a matter of fact — becalmed, tinkering with the motor I'd delayed having fixed. But you can't sail without wind, and this morning I had none.

He was a rather grizzled fellow, not unlike his boat, which had clearly seen better days. The bottom of his boat, I saw as he pulled alongside me, was covered with catfish and perch. It looked like the catfish ranged in size from three pounds to as much as fifteen pounds.

"Stalled out?" he asked me.

"Becalmed," I told him. "I haven't had to use the motor for a couple of days, and I've put off getting it fixed."

"Motors," he said. "I don't like 'em much either, but all

in all, they're handy things to have. Need a lift to town?"

"I'll accept that offer," I told him, "if the wind doesn't come up. If it does, I'll be all right." I gestured at his catch. "Some of those fish look pretty big."

"It's my living," he told me. "I throw the small ones back. Got lines strung for six miles up and down the river. I'm just tending to 'em."

It seemed a better way to make a living than some I could think of, and I envied the man the beauty of his working conditions. I could not help but think of the many years I'd spent working in an environment that I intensely disliked. This seemed to be a man who had chosen his job out of preference rather than from necessity. I told him so.

"Fishin's all I've ever known," he told me. "But I'll say this — at day's end, you can sure see the results of your labors."

"What's a good day?" I asked him.

"About two hundred pounds," he said. I told him that I would certainly, even in my limited fishing experience, have to agree with that.

I could have talked to the fisherman longer. He was yet another in the succession of people I'd met on the river who seemed to know who he was. I wondered, of course, if this was what I was in the process of finding out about myself, with the help of *White Knuckles* and the water. Then the wind came up, and I was on my way again. Perhaps that wind, coming up when it did, was an answer in itself.

At the Russellville boat dock and marina, I put in and sent the motor off to be repaired. I've decided I'll need it on occasion. With a motor and sails, I'll have the best of both worlds.

The countryside has become much more mountainous here, and pine trees and cedars can now be seen in abundance on both sides of me. The good November weather has persisted. It's been seventy-two degrees today, and even tonight the temperature sits on a high sixty. I didn't have as much time to contemplate all of this as I thought I might, though. The Stinkpot returned, repaired. I'm ready to go again at first light.

Tomorrow offers potentially tough sailing, and I'll need that motor. It's a half-mile to Dardanelle Lock, and then the chart shows a long, narrow, winding stretch of river with no lakes all the way to Little Rock. That's eighty-four miles and three locks from here. I'll put up the mainsail to help that little motor out, but it's going to be mostly motoring tomorrow.

As for the hunters, I found out in Russellville that deer season is open. Rifle shots ought to be the order of the day tomorrow, and I sure hope that nobody tries his marksmanship on *White Knuckles's* mast.

November 20
Mile 178, Arkansas River

It was all motor today — twenty-eight miles through a dead calm and drizzling rain. It wasn't much progress, but it was better than none at all. We reached Lock Nine at 1530, and I decided that I would wait until morning before locking through. This has been a tough one.

But I did find a pretty little cove adjacent to the dam where I could snub *White Knuckles* up to an overhanging tree, stern anchor out. That's where I'm sitting now, looking out over the water. There are ducks around me, safe from hunters for the night. It's very peaceful here.

One thing I've become thankful for during the past days is that I've never been a finicky eater. God knows how I would have fared out here if I had been. I've purchased mostly prepared foods like soups, vegetables, stews, chili, and canned meats. I eat my share of Mug-o-Lunches®, too — anything that's simple. I don't get involved with glass-enclosed foods because a sailboat isn't too kind to them.

I keep eggs, cheese, bacon, potatoes, onions, and a few other perishables in the bilge. They keep well down there, especially at this time of year. My milk is made from powder, with one teaspoon of vanilla added per quart for a little flavor. My diet sounds bland, I know, but eating is just not a priority out here.

In fact, I always eat my lunch in the cockpit while under way — crackers and cheese, a thermos of soup, perhaps a boiled egg. It's the journey that's important.

As for cooking, I've learned a few tricks. I boil eggs by bringing the water to a boil, covering the pan, and setting it aside for about twenty minutes. They finish cooking at their leisure this way, and they're much easier to peel. *White Knuckles* has a two-burner alcohol stove, but I've never used it. Instead I prefer the little one-burner, propane camp stove that I brought along; it's faster and much more economical.

For breakfast, I eat cereal and toast, which I cook in a skillet. For stews or beans, I use a small pressure cooker. I'm told that one can even bake bread in such a pressure cooker, and I'll try it someday. But I have found that a stew will keep fresh in the pressure cooker, provided the pressure cap is left on, for several days of fairly good eating.

Shopping is accomplished by hitching a ride into a nearby town or by walking there. This is the off season for the marinas down the Arkansas, so it's tough to find some of the things I really need. We make do, though, *White Knuckles* and I.

It's not only the off season for the marinas, it's also vacation time for insects, which delights me. I haven't seen so much as a mosquito out here, and that's just fine by me. There are many things to recommend taking this kind of trip at this time of year, and the absence of flying, biting critters is one of those things. By the way, another reason is that the hurricane season ends in the gulf after October.

November 21
Mile 157, Arkansas River
(Toad Suck Ferry Lock)

The rains came. In fact, that's an understatement. We arrived at tonight's stop in a driving, blinding storm that made for plenty of rough going. But here we are, about half a mile from Toad Suck Ferry Lock. How do you like that for a name?

I would have tried to negotiate the lock before calling it quits today, but there were two tows backed up awaiting lockage, and I was wet and tired. So was *White Knuckles.* It's bliss to get into some dry clothes, have some hot food, and just sit back and relax.

The day didn't start this badly. This morning was windy with just a few sprinkles of rain. There was a bad mishap, however. I had the companionway doors lying on the cabin hatch, with the chart book on top of them, when a sudden gust of wind took all the charts overboard. The water was turbulent because of the storm, and it took me three jibes to rescue my precious guidebook. I was sure it would be ruined, but despite the fact that it feels like an old dishrag, it's still usable. It was another lesson learned the hard way, but I'll never leave my charts like that again — you can bet on that! I even lost my hat in the rescue process.

The White River will take us to the Mississippi, and I've reflected several times today on a conversation I had with a fellow back in Russellville. He was a good deal older than I, but in some ways he was my alter ego. This man, you see, had been boating down the Mississippi.

He strongly advised me to go no further.

Did he scare me? Yes, he scared me. He told me he had met tows on the lower Mississippi that were nine barges wide and nine barges long. The largest I've seen so far were three barges wide and five or six long. He told me that the wake from these huge tows was ten feet high and came over his cabin top. And what kind of boat did he have?

A twenty-seven-foot, Chris Craft Cruiser with twin engines.

"Look," I told him, not sure I believed myself, "my boat can take those wakes better than a flat-bottomed cabin cruiser."

"No small boat can take those things," he replied. "Not without finally cracking up."

The conversation had become a little heated, which puzzled me. Why should this older fellow be so resentful of my trip down the river?

"Did you lose your boat?" I asked him, assuming this was the reason for his hostility.

"I lost more'n that," he said mysteriously. I could see that I would be getting that and nothing else out of him.

I have to hope that he exaggerated in the telling of his tale, because I know that I am going on. As for the wakes: if meet them we must, then meet them we will.

But his words stay with me like a portent, perhaps, or some dire warning. Have I attempted too much? With my entrance to the Mississippi, will my smooth sailing be over? Tonight, here in the cold and the rain, only the wind replies.

November 22
Mile 121, Arkansas River
(Little Rock)

This, of course, is an anniversary. Sixteen years ago today, a President was shot down in Dallas. Like most people who were around for that tragedy, I remember so well what I was doing and where I was on that day. I know equally well that, sixteen years ago, I never would have thought that on this November 22 I'd be living out an adventure that had been only a dream.

Not that I got the opportunity for much in the way of adventure today. We're anchored just above the Missouri-Pacific Railroad drawbridge tonight, just outside Little Rock. We would have gone farther, to a marina about a mile down the river where I had hoped to tie up, but the drawbridge operator failed to hear that airhorn of mine — poor thing that it is — so we're stuck for tonight.

One thing this journey has definitely taught me is that *White Knuckles* needs a bigger horn. Nobody — not lockmasters, not tugboat pilots, and certainly not anyone on a boat — has been able to hear this little toot of ours. In fact, we'll probably have to follow a tugboat through that drawbridge in the morning, and there are two more drawbridges before we get through Little Rock, none of them automated.

This was a day of loss, as is perhaps appropriate for any November 22. For starters, I deep-sixed the boat's fancy indoor-outdoor carpet. I hadn't been able to keep it dry, and I hadn't been able to dry it when it got wet. Frankly, it was starting to stink. Now I'm working on a fiberglass cabin floor, and I must say it's far better. Things slide around more, but it's clean, and I can keep it clean.

Our other loss was an anchor and about a hundred feet of line. This wasn't intentional; in fact, it was far from it. It was the result of a run-in with a speedboat.

I'd been carrying this particular anchor on the bow pulpit, lashed on with some cord I could cut easily, allowing me to drop anchor pretty much instantly. Along toward noon today, we met a zippy little speedboat about twenty feet long, which, to tell the truth, didn't look all that formidable. Its wake was, admittedly, larger than that of many tows, but it still didn't look so bad.

So much for my judgment of wakes! Its two wakes rebounded from each shore, meeting right under *White Knuckles's* bow. The anchor broke loose.

I didn't see it, but I did suddenly hear twenty feet of chain passing through the house pipe. I tried to stop it. Without even thinking, I dashed forward and tried to hold onto the rope, but I couldn't slow it or even take a turn around the cleat with it. It smoked right through both my gloves, and the bitter end of the chain kissed my knee good-bye with a final, sharp slap. As I stood there feeling like a fool, watching my rope descend into the river, this thought occurred to me — now I know why they call it the bitter end.

I shouldn't have run for the bow like that. Instead, I should have turned the boat or cut the engines. But we were really making time, with the motor at about three-fourths throttle in a strong current and a following wind. In the heat of action, I overreacted. I can't afford to do that any more.

Someone may find my anchor and return it. If that doesn't happen, I'll have to buy a new one in Little Rock. But that's all right. I want to lay up there for a few days, stock the boat and clean it, and look up an old friend. His name is Wills, and he and I put in a long time in the postal service together. He lives in Little Rock now, and it's been fifteen years since I've seen him. He's going to be very surprised to see me.

November 23

I learned today why nobody could hear my horn from the drawbridge last evening, and the knowledge made me feel pretty silly. There are no operators at these drawbridges; they're controlled by a fellow sitting in an office in downtown Little Rock. I wasn't kidding when I said they weren't automated. In fact, they're not even manned.

And how did I finally manage to get this information? I started the day by giving chase to a tow of barges, hoping to go under the drawbridges — all of them — on his coattails. But his backwash was too heavy, and with our limited horsepower, *White Knuckles* and I quickly fell behind. We saw the drawbridge go up, and we saw it go down just moments before we finally got there.

So we circled around and around for about two hours,

giving two short blasts on the horn from time to time, but with no results. How could there be? No one was up there to hear, and, worse than falling on deaf ears, my toots were falling on no ears at all. Finally, we gave up and went back upstream to a dredge we'd passed earlier. We got permission to tie alongside. Then the dredge operator and I sat down for a little talk. This is when I learned about these remote-control drawbridges and found out that the only way to get the bridge raised is through contact with the home office by radio or telephone.

Here I was without radio or telephone. What's a poor-boy sailor to do?

The dredge operator took pity on me and contacted the bridge operator. I was advised that I could pass under at 1606. And that is how I came to be at the first drawbridge at precisely that time. Both of the first two bridges, which are operated by the Missouri-Pacific Railroad, use the same system, and both are controlled by the same fellow sitting in Little Rock. The third one uses this system, too, but it's operated by Rock Island. I'll be calling them from the marina when *White Knuckles* and I depart.

For at least a day or two, it's time to relax. I can't leave the tiller for more than a minute when I'm steering down the waterway. That is confining. The marked channel crosses and recrosses the river constantly, and the current is seldom on the stern; it may quarter the beam on either side or even be beam on. Thus, the tiller must be attended constantly, and this constant attention is wearing. I would guess even old sailors get tired of it.

The wind, too, can work against us at the same time the

current does, causing the boat to come about or head for shore very quickly. There are strong countercurrents too, in that river, and they always mean trouble. They can be spotted by noticing an eddy in the water — one of those little whirlpools that become visible from time to time. Even the motion of driftwood and scum on the water can provide clues. But it takes watching — all the time. This has been a wonderful trip so far, but it hasn't been easy; it has called for constant vigilance. Even now, tied up in North Little Rock and supposedly taking it easy, I find myself watching the water. There's a current flowing upstream that is fully as strong as the main one only two or three hundred feet away. And what do I see working in between the two? A huge whirlpool!

I sat down early this evening for a good, long talk with Jim Simpson, the proprietor of the marina here. He's been at his job a long time and knows the river well.

"Back in Russellville," I told him, "I talked with a fellow who warned me about ten-foot-high wakes on the Mississippi."

"You should have asked him what he was drinking out there," Simpson replied. "I never saw one over four feet."

"That sounds more like it," I said, with relief in my voice. "I'm too new at this to be up for anything ten feet high."

"Look," Simpson told me, "you'll be on a bigger river. The effect of the wakes is going to be reduced by the strong current, to start with. Then there's the greater width of the river. Gives you more room to get away from a big wake."

I thanked him and hoped he was right. Both he and the fellow near Russellville appeared to be old salts, but who do you trust?

NOVEMBER 24 AND 25

Howard Wills had put on some weight over the past fifteen years. I'd called him yesterday from the marina, but he wasn't able to make it over to the boat until today. Even then, his arrival was a bit of a surprise. He just popped in as I was carrying a couple of armloads of groceries on board.

"Howard," I told him, "it's great to see you. Welcome to my home away from home. This is *White Knuckles.*"

Howard, never a small man, clearly felt cramped. "You live on this thing?" he asked me. "Or do you just sail from motel to motel?"

I laughed. "Nope. I sleep here. The truth is, this boat sleeps five."

"Five what? Monkeys?"

We both laughed then. I could tell that Howard, like most of my friends back home, was perplexed by my dual freedom and confinement. I offered him coffee.

"Forget that," he told me. "You're about to be the proud recipient of a home-cooked meal, and it damn sure looks like you could use one. Going to turn me down?"

"No way," I told him. "I'm right behind you."

We drove to Howard's home in Little Rock where I met Betty, his wife. She was gracious to me, and the way that she and Howard embraced when she met us at the door told me most of what anyone needed to know about their marriage; it was a good one, and they were still in love.

Over drinks, Betty asked me about the journey so far.

"Not easy," I told her. "But fulfilling. The most fulfilling thing I've ever done."

Betty smiled at her husband. "Want me to pack you a bag, Howard?" she asked him.

Howard laughed his good laugh again. "Are you kidding?" he told her. "There isn't room!"

Betty turned back to me. "Actually," I told her, "there is, but it's hard to find when the boat is packed. There are five bunks, but I think that's more an advertising gimmick than anything else." I explained that the "V" berths in the bow are good for storage and not much else.

"Believe me, I've got them filled, too. The starboard berths are in similar shape," I told them. "I've got a dirty-clothes bag, boots, shoes, and wet-weather gear on one, and under the other one are tools. The forward port berth holds chart books and an extra five-gallon water container. That just leaves an after-port berth for me."

"You'll have to translate some of that," she told me. "I'm not up on 'port' and 'after-port.'"

"What I'm really trying to say is that I am crowded on there," I told her. "I probably overstocked, but the first time, how do you know?"

"Sounds like you've packed wall to wall," Howard said. "You probably have trouble even finding your electrical outlets."

"Electricity?" I laughed. "I'm roughing it, Howard!"

We had another round of drinks and then sat down to a meal which I thought at the time was the most sumptuous I'd ever eaten. I realize now that I was looking at this meal from the vantage point of weeks of cheese sandwiches, but I still believe it would have been wonderful under any circumstances. We had baked ham, beans, potato salad, corn, and rolls, all topped off with homemade apple pie with ice cream. It was the first meal I had eaten ashore since my adventure began.

Finally, I pushed back from the table. "I think I've made a pig of myself," I admitted.

"Nonsense," Betty told me. "Another piece of pie?"

"Where would I put it?" I winced. "The most overcrowded thing on that boat tonight is going to be my stomach."

By this time it was 1800, and though the skies had been grim all day, they now seemed to be clearing. Tomorrow would be a good day, I hoped, for getting under way.

Even so, as I sat at this pleasant suburban dinner table, the remains of a fine meal before us, I could not help but be homesick. There was indeed much love between Howard and Betty, and, as we talked of old friends and current plans, I couldn't help but envy their sense of complacency, their obvious feeling that they had arrived at the place where they wanted to be.

I excused myself and asked to use their telephone. Howard led me to the bedroom extension, rightly sensing that I preferred some privacy for this call.

I dialed the familiar area code and number. What would she be doing at six o'clock on a weekday evening? I knew too well — arriving home from work and starting to think about some dinner.

To my relief, she accepted the collect call. "Is anything wrong?" she asked me. Her first question showed her wifely concern about her husband's welfare.

"I'm fine," I told her. "I'm even full. I'm with Howard and Betty Wills in Little Rock, and they've just fed me a grand meal."

"And the boat?" she asked.

"At the marina," I said. "Shipshape."

"So you're going on." She didn't sound openly disappointed, but her words probably didn't come out as cheery as she wanted them to, either.

"Yeah," I told her. "I'm under way again tomorrow."

We talked about practical things for a bit, and then I said, "I miss you. Dinner with Howard and Betty made me think about everything I've left behind."

"I miss you, too," she said. "And I'm lonely."

"You know I have to do this, don't you?"

"I know you think you do."

"Will you meet me? In New Orleans?"

She said nothing for a moment. Then, "We'll have to see. There's work."

"I want you to," I told her. "Very much."

I hung up that phone with a pit of loneliness in my gut. For the second time on this journey, I wanted to chuck it all, get out on the highway, and catch a ride back home. I cautioned myself to stay away from evenings with happily married couples in the future if I wanted to keep going. Such evenings were too reminiscent of all I'd left behind.

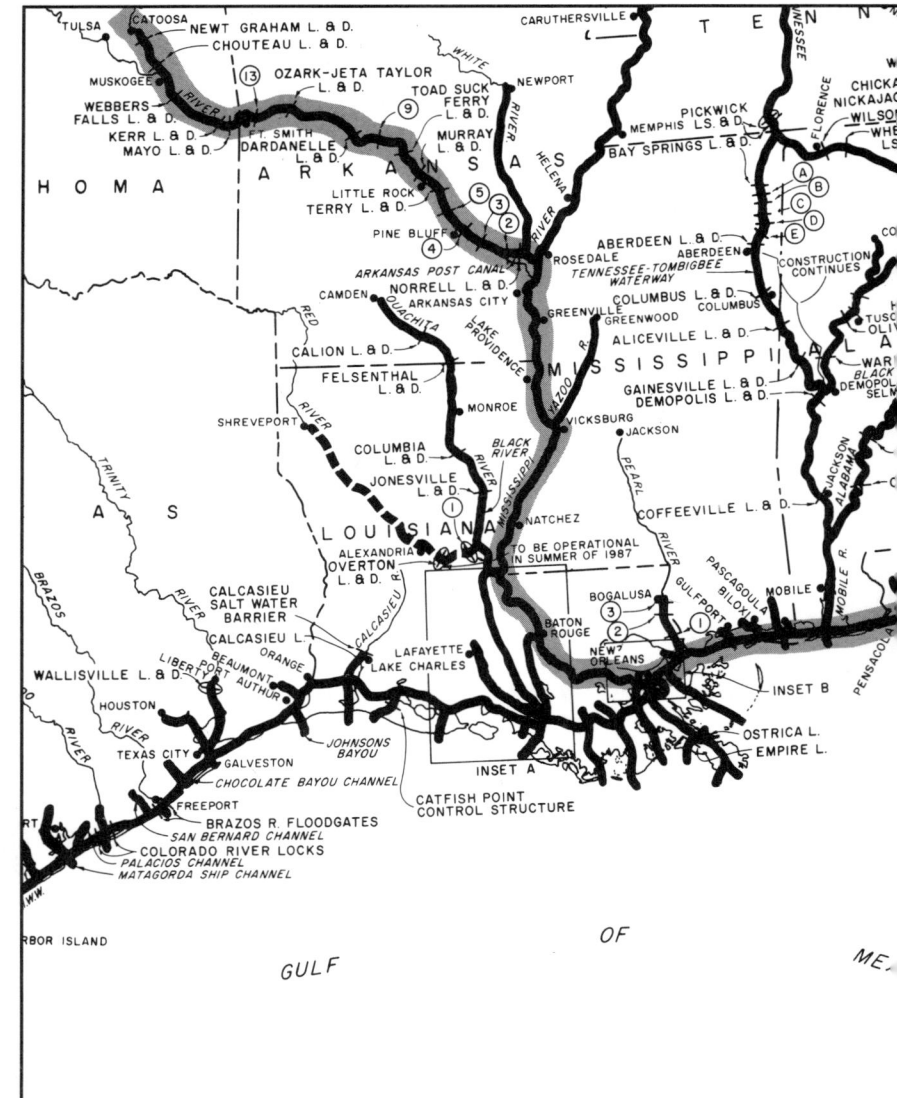

**November 3–March 20
Voyage of *White Knuckles***

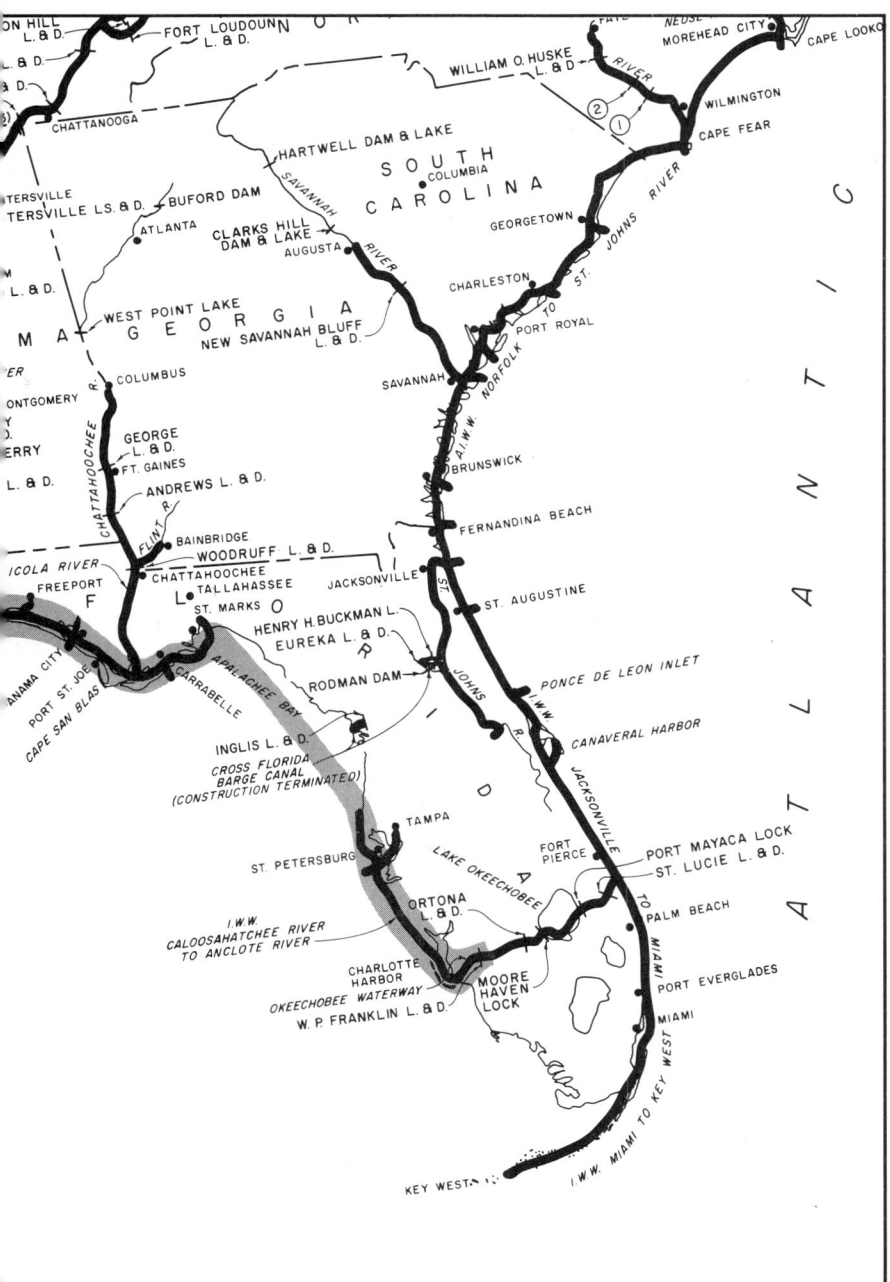

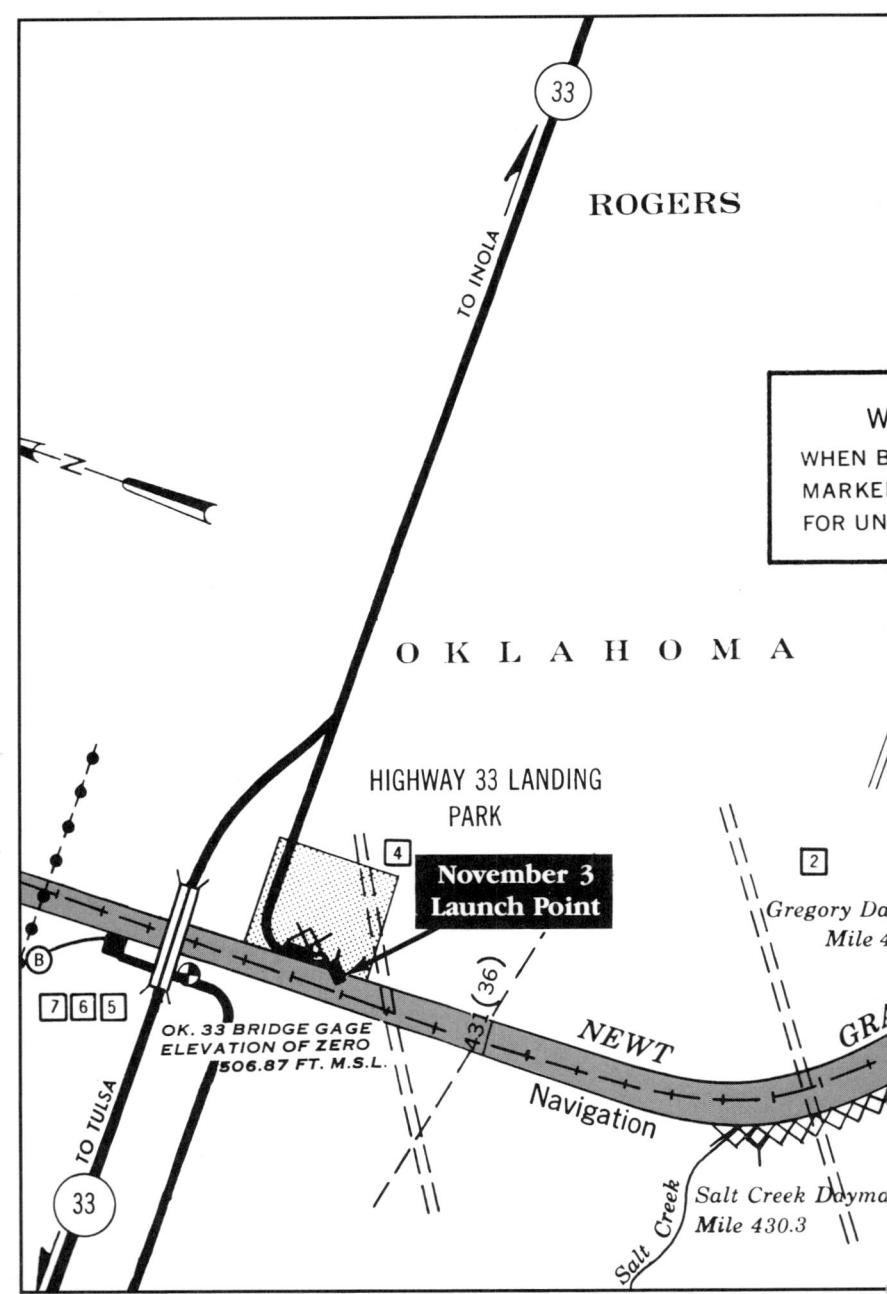

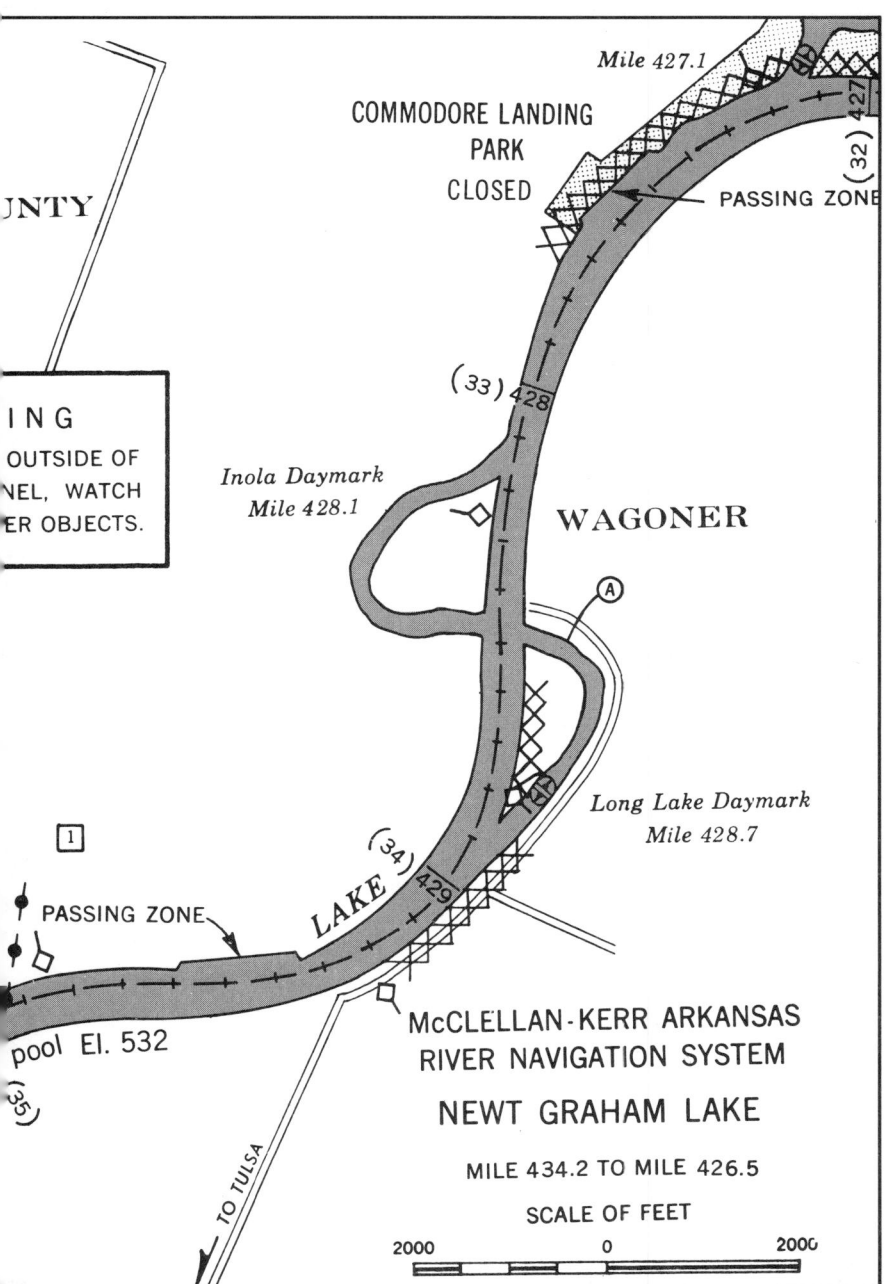

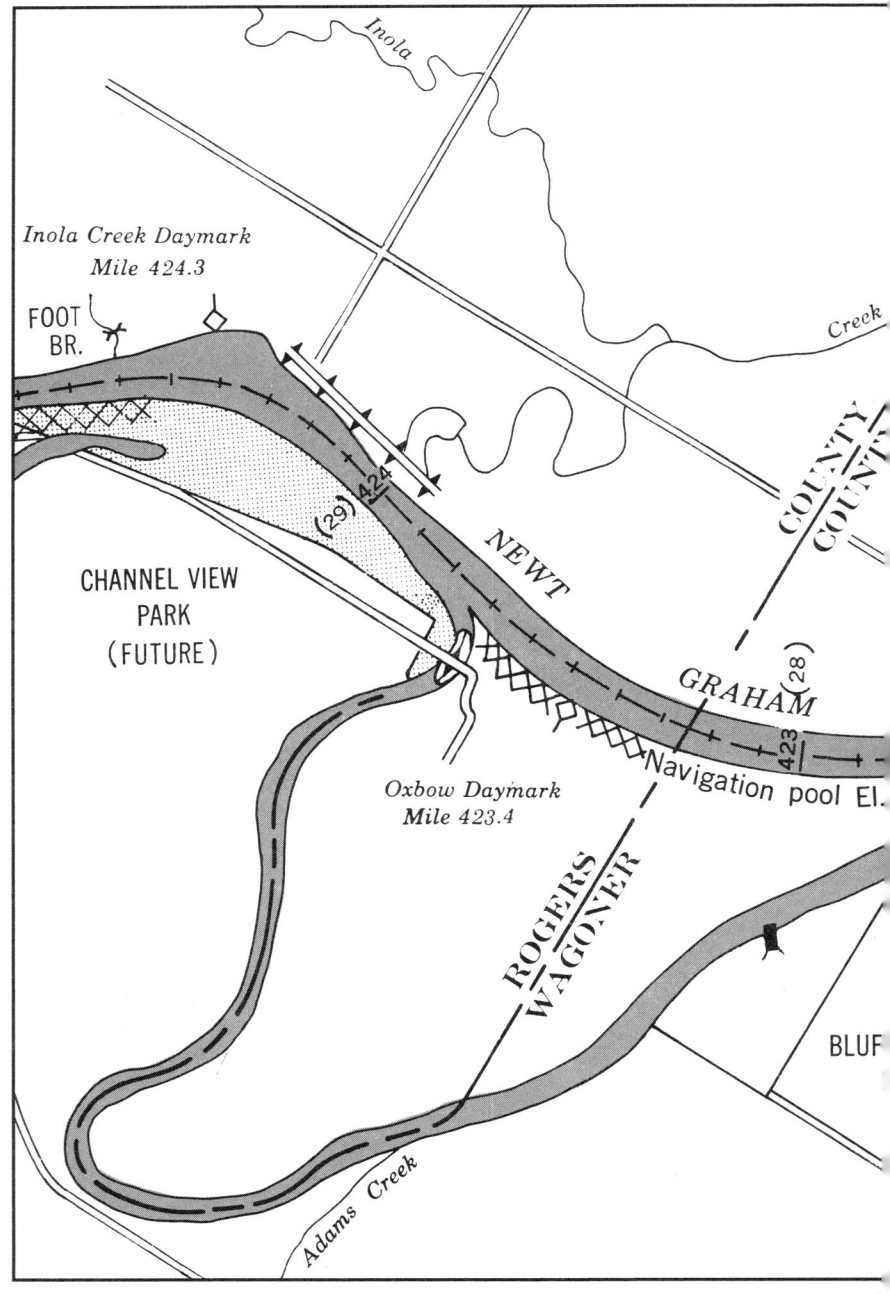

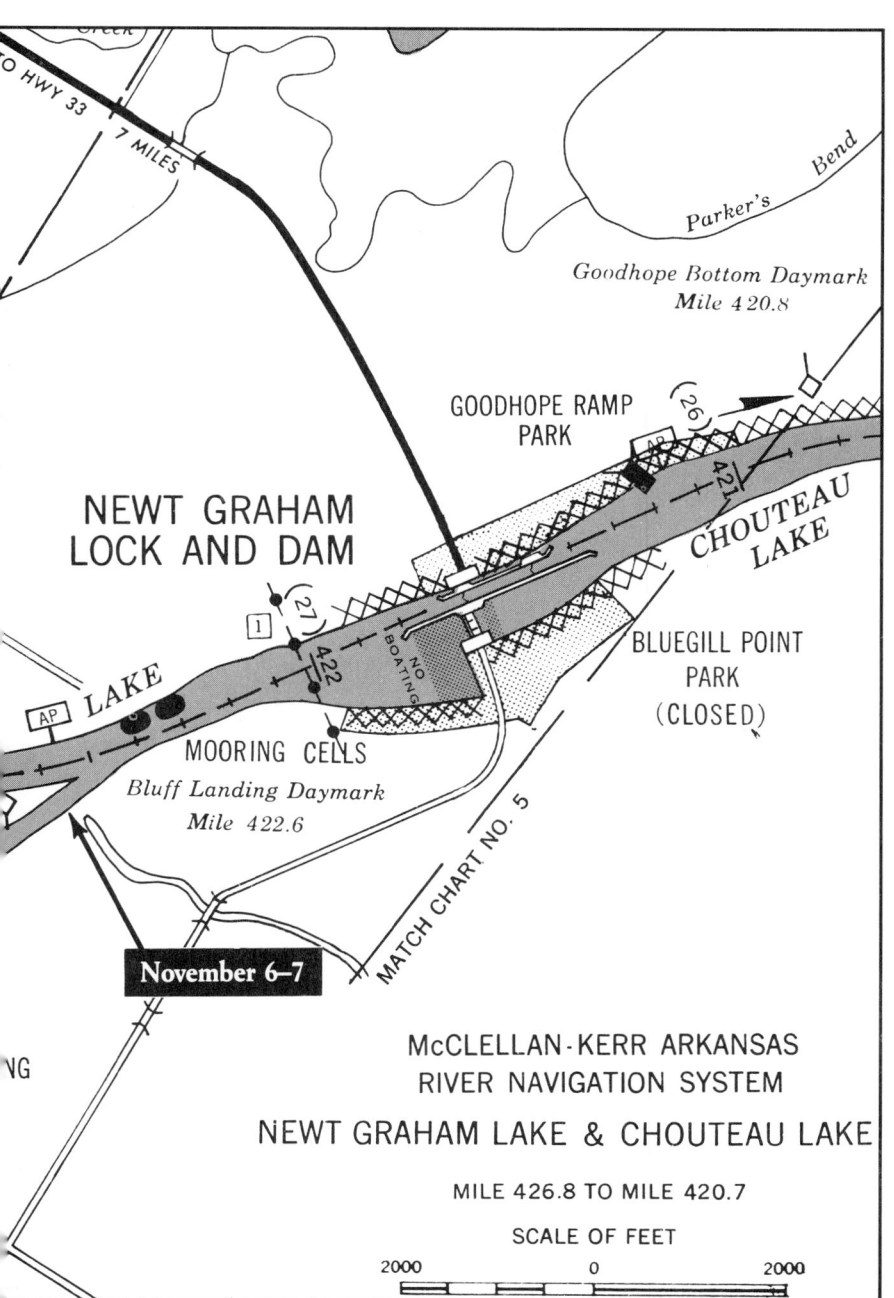

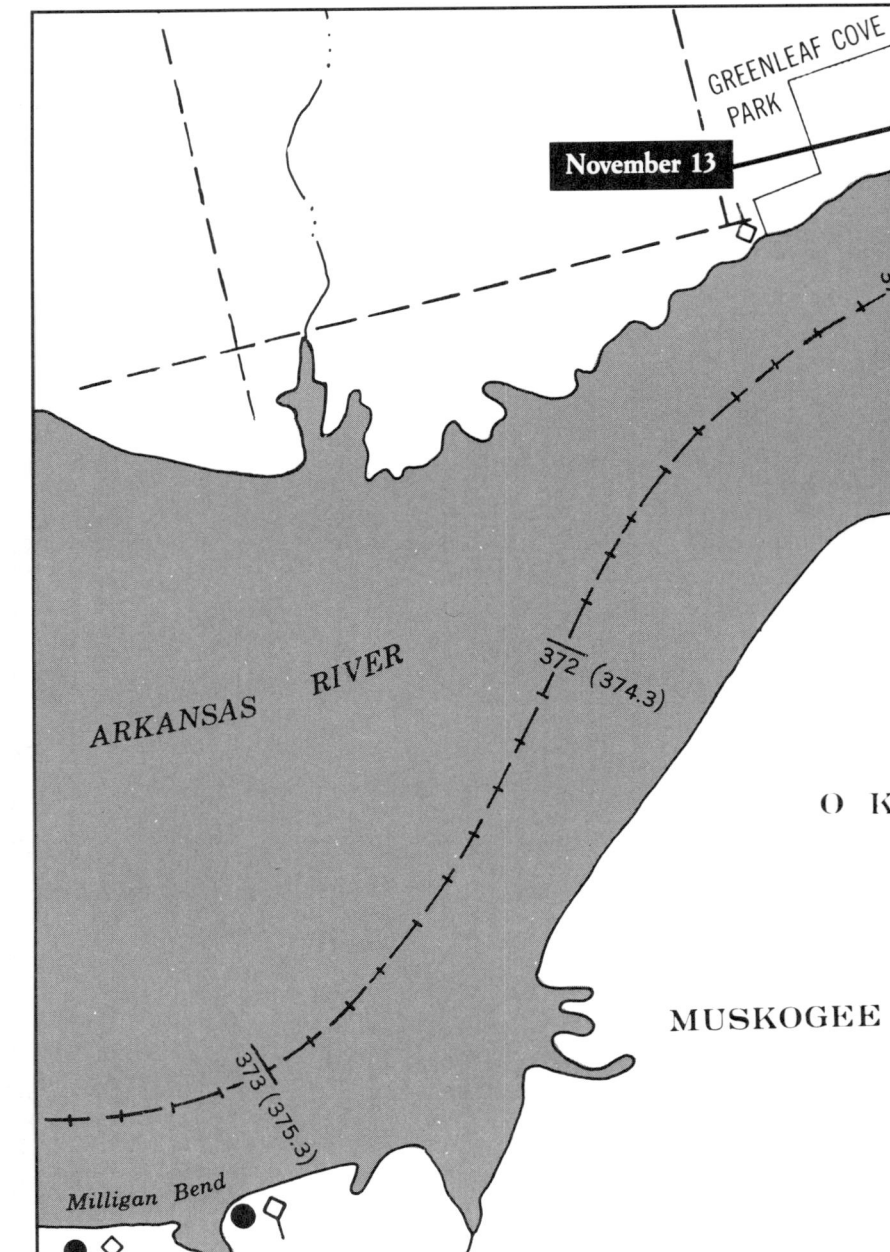

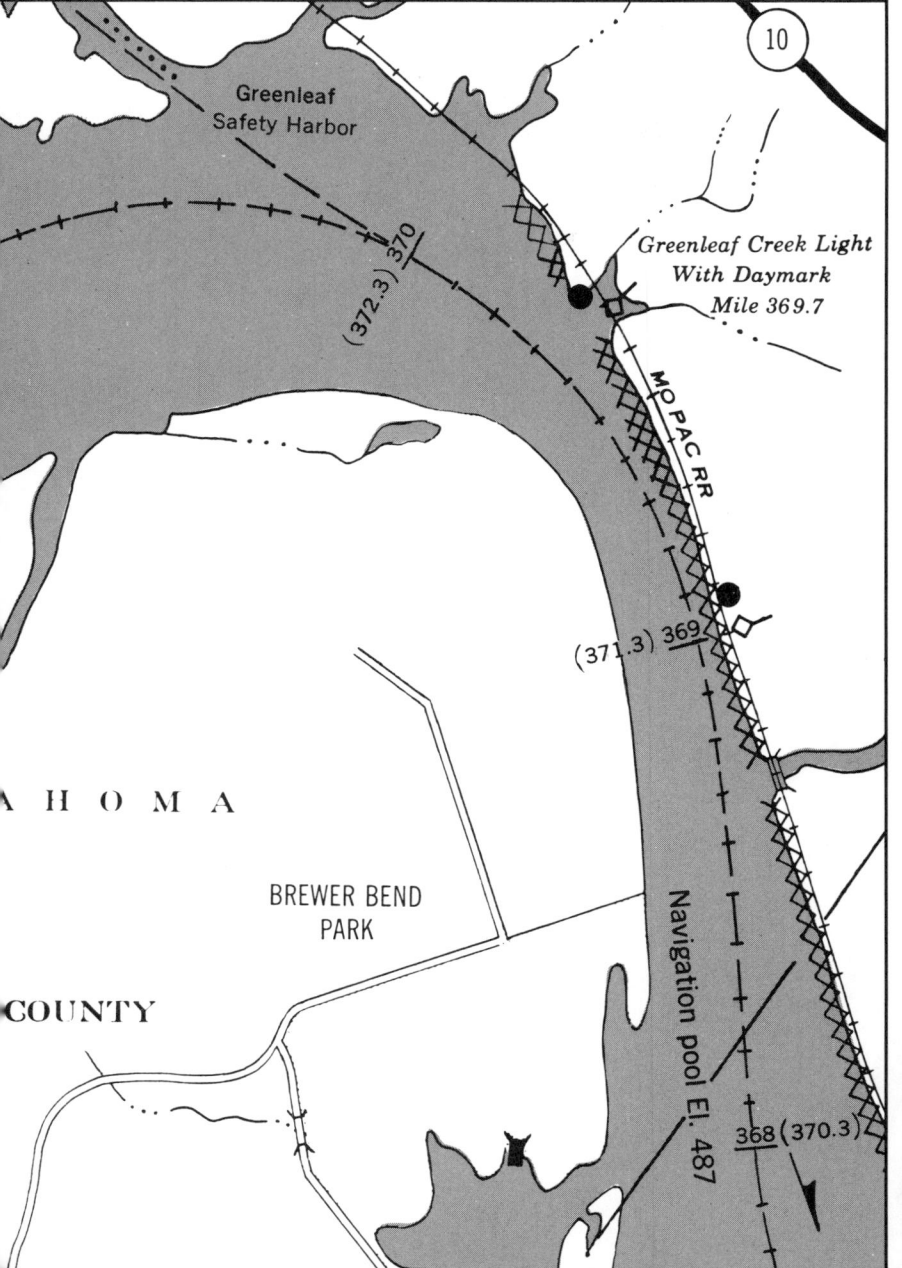

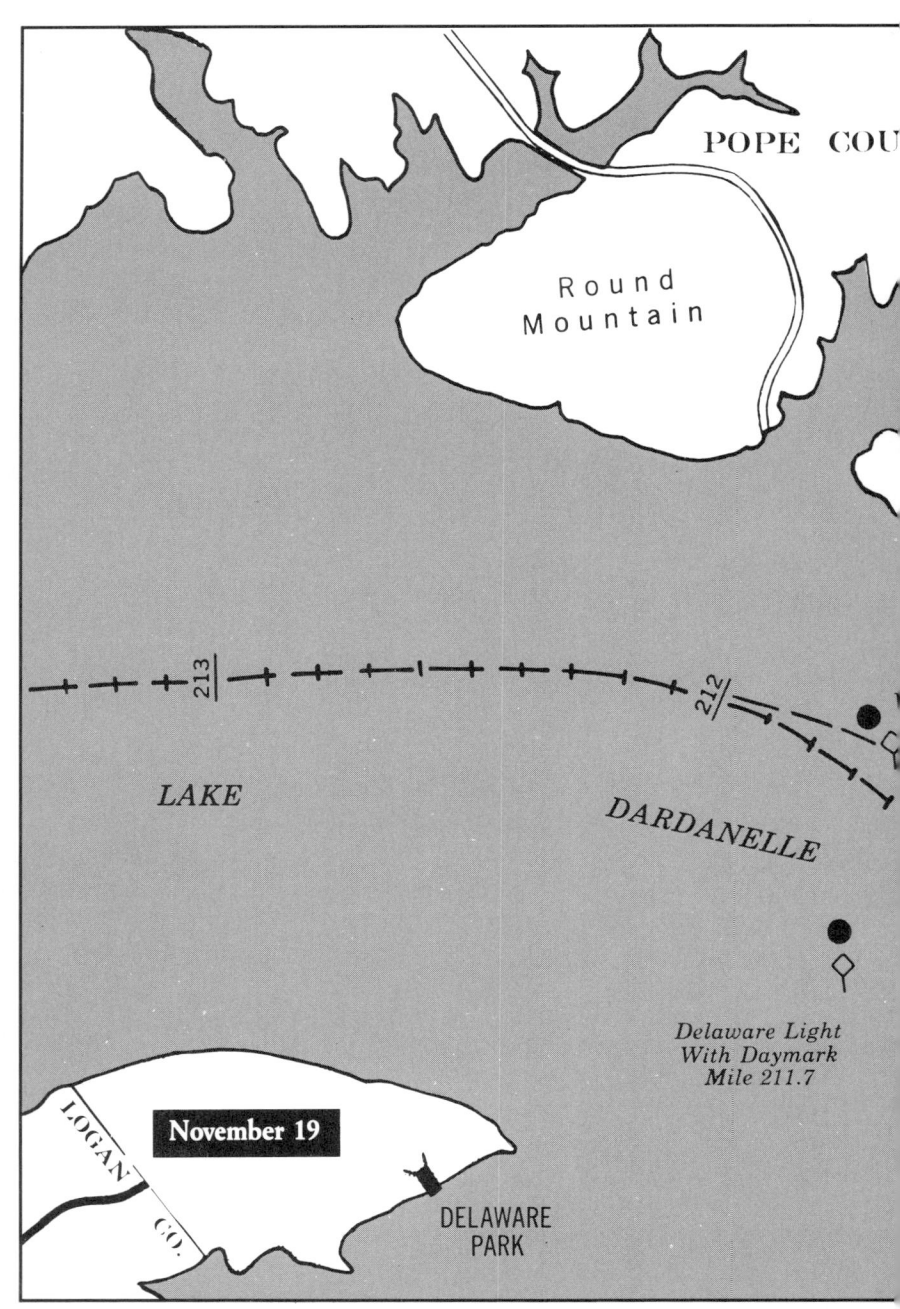

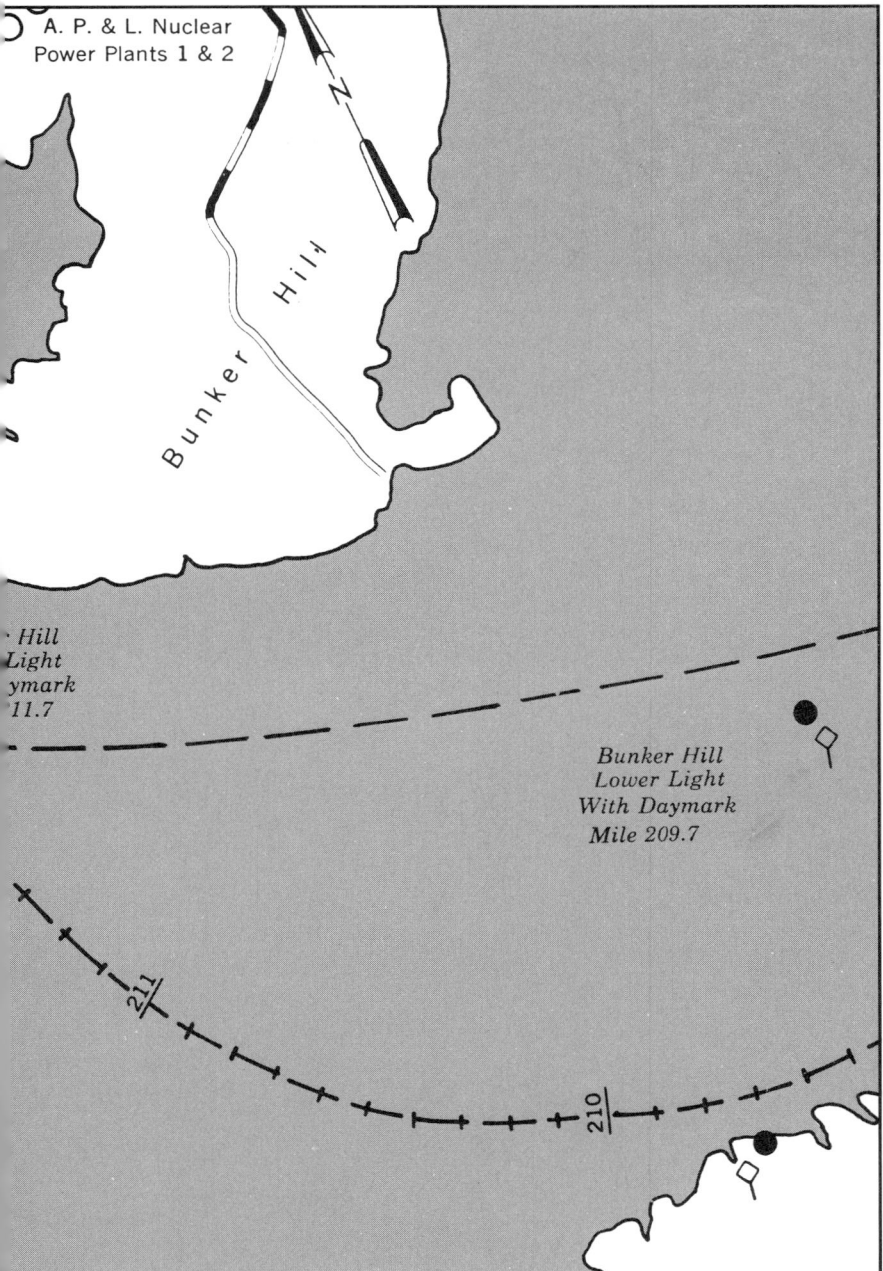

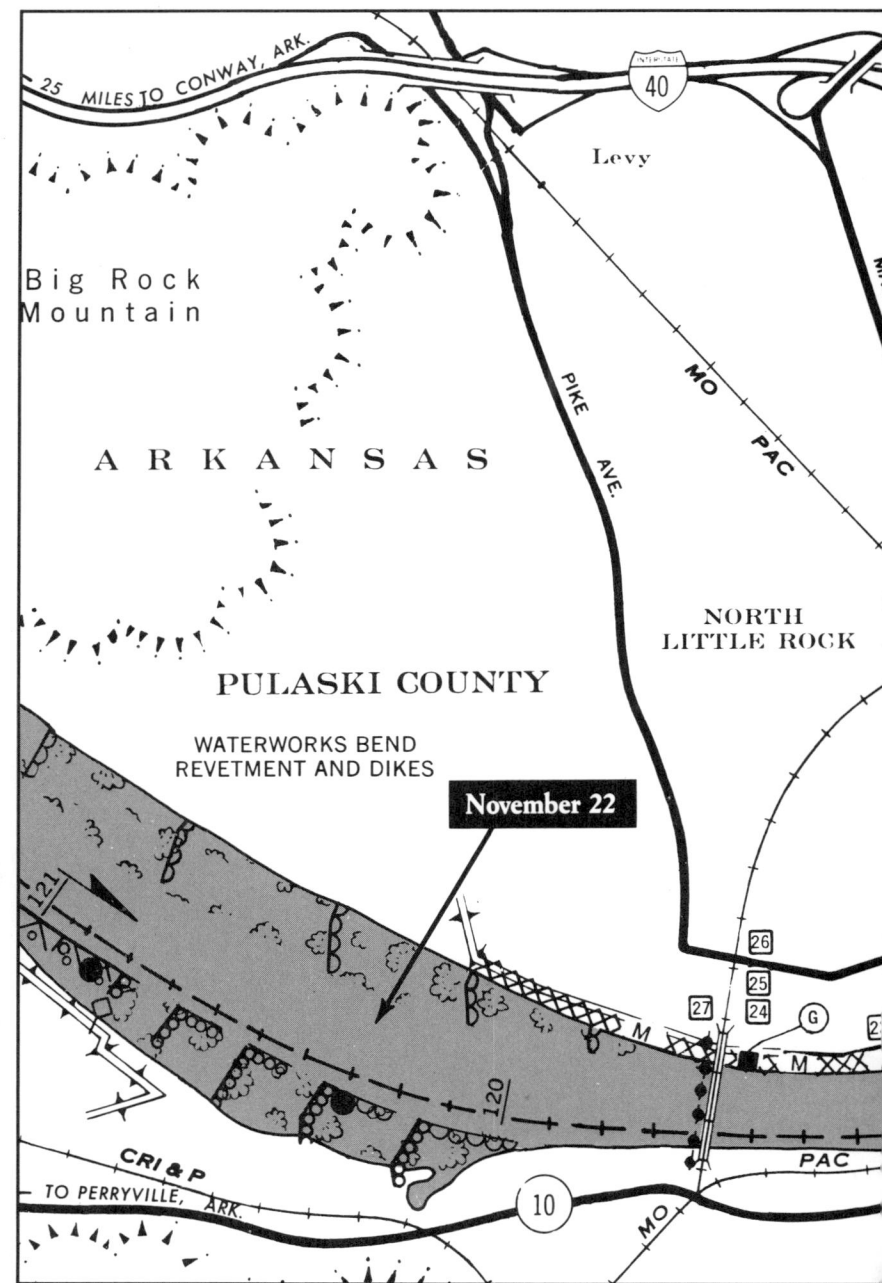

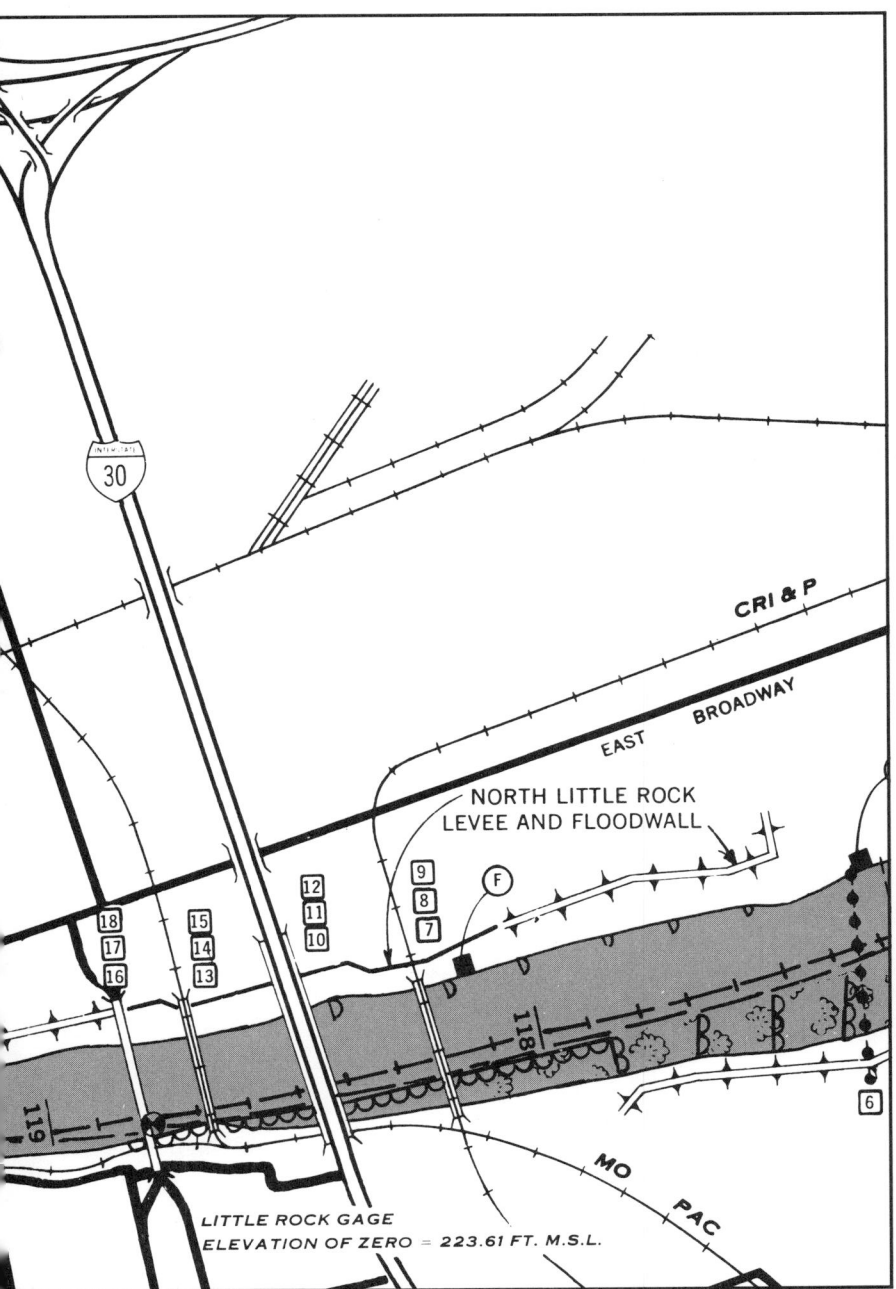

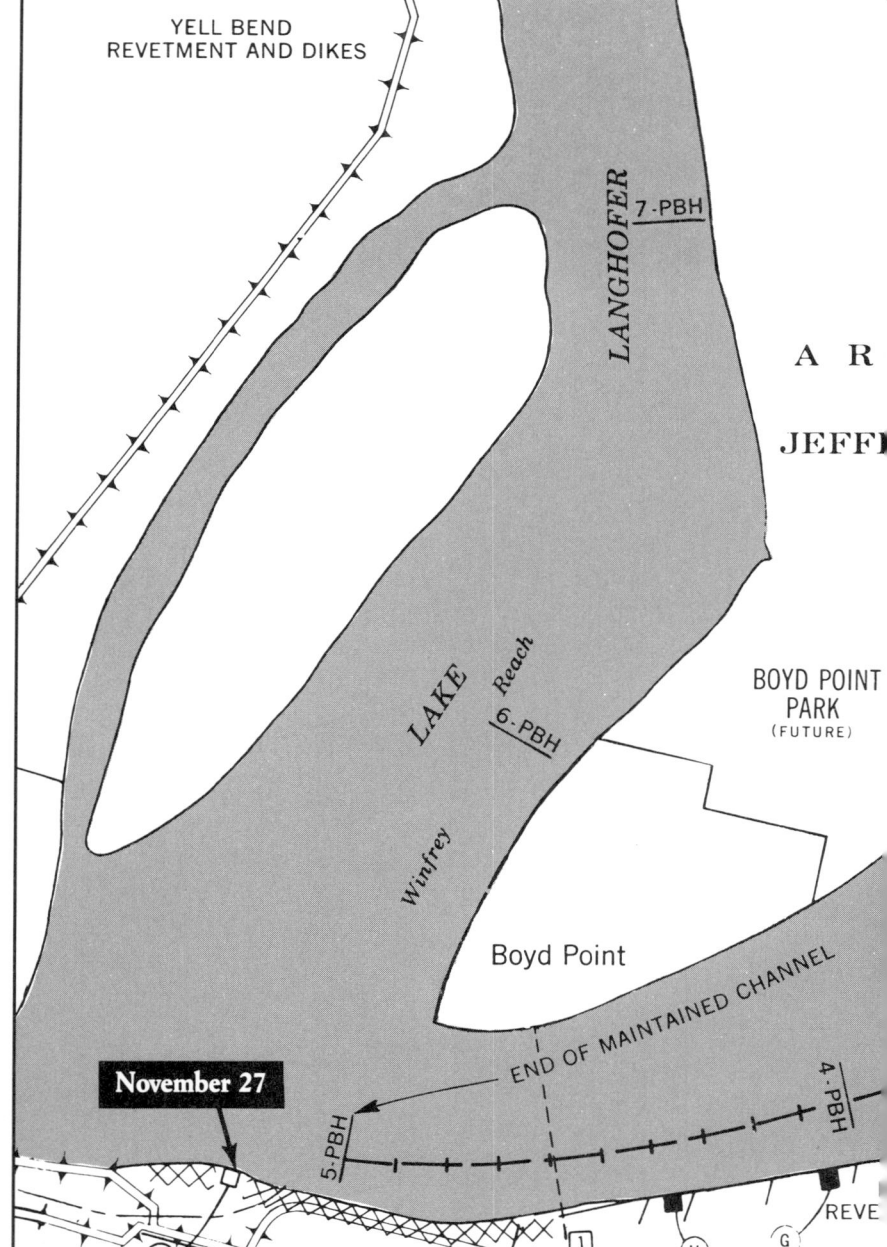

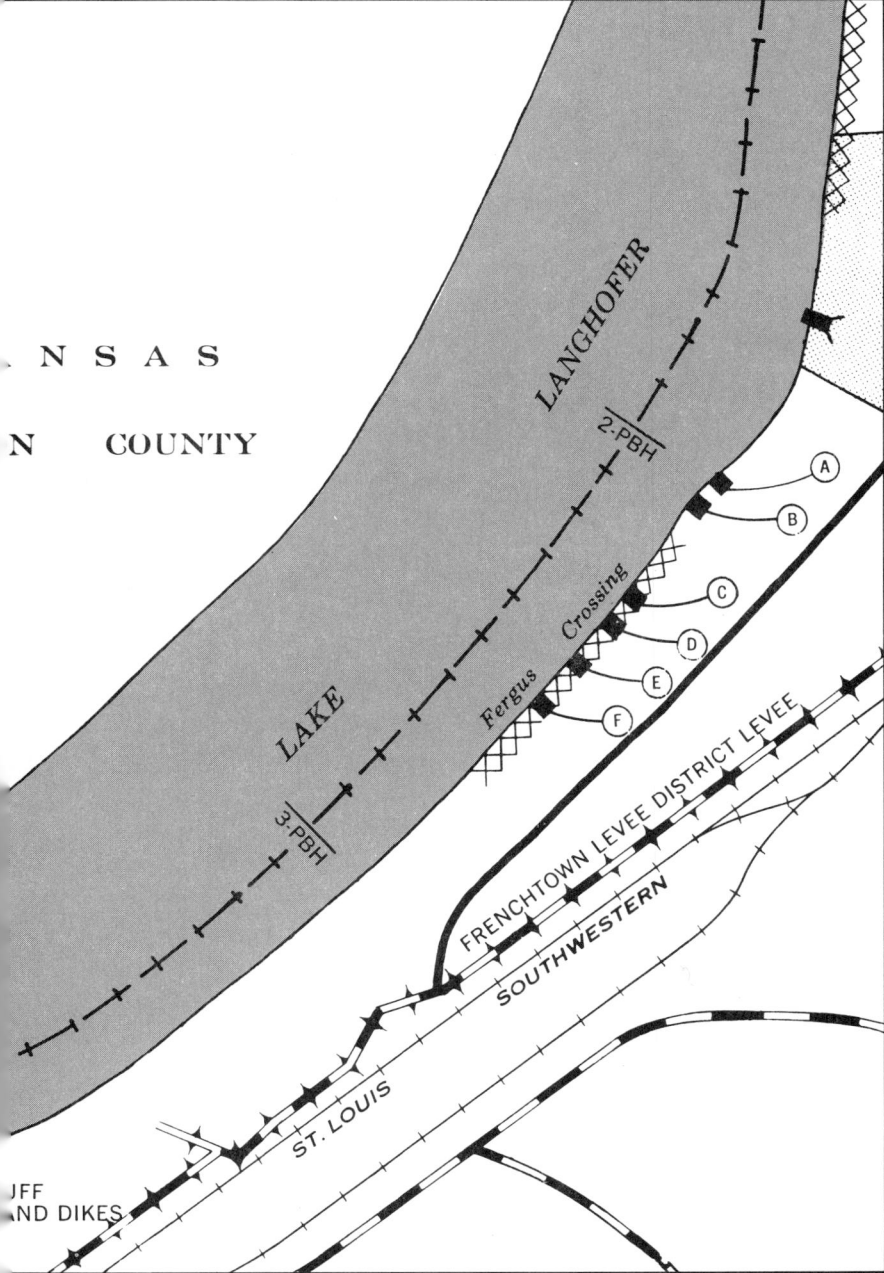

November 26
Mile 78, Arkansas River

The river changed today. It grew wider and swifter, and the current became downright unpredictable. Though the wind was calm all day and the temperature got above seventy degrees, the river itself seemed to be in great turmoil. There were eddies, reverse currents, and countless small whirlpools. At times, I looked at the water ahead and was surprised to see that it seemed to be boiling. Today, the river seemed full of signs and portents.

White Knuckles felt it, too. I could feel her hesitate at times, and then at other times, she veered sharply for no apparent reason. Her little motor would lug down suddenly, and then, just as suddenly, it would run free again. She clearly knows that she's in unfamiliar territory.

I tried both sides of the channel, but I could find no steady current. The river bottom along here must be horribly eroded and pockmarked to cause such stir in the water. For an entire thirty-mile stretch, the current persisted in this manner. It's been our roughest haul on the trip thus far.

Still deeply affected by my dinner with Howard and Betty and by my phone call home yesterday, I spent much of today's journey a little distracted, my thoughts often with my wife. But I don't want to feel homesick now — I want no second thoughts. So I willed myself to think instead of the conversation I had with Jim Simpson, the fellow who ran the marina back in Little Rock. He had recently made a trip up the river in his own boat and had plenty of good information for me. He even went through my Mississippi chart book and made corrections; in addition, he marked some anchorages for me. He claimed that things were going to get rougher on the Mississippi because it has a seven-miles-per-hour current as opposed to the two- or three-miles-per-hour current of the Arkansas. I don't believe he mentioned the stretch I went through today. That might have made him consider the Arkansas to be more formidable.

Some of the information about the process of anchoring has already become pertinent. Places to anchor seem to be getting harder and harder to find now, even though the river is wider. We're anchored tonight just out of the channel — but we're in a fairly strong current. I remember that Jim Simpson had told me, above all else, to use two anchors.

"I do use two," I'd told him. "But I guess I don't know the full reason for doing so."

"It's because of the beavers," Jim had replied with a grin. "They'll eat right through an anchor line in the middle of the night. That's no joke."

"I should be using three!" I'd protested. "If they'll eat one, then surely they'll eat through two!"

Jim had laughed at that. "A good point," he'd said. "Although you'd be sailing pretty top-heavy."

Jim Simpson had also told me that on the Mississippi I'm going to have to anchor, when I can, behind an island or a peninsula for protection against the barge traffic and the immense wakes. Jim and his boat were set ashore by one of those wakes on his last trip.

Tonight I sit on the deck relaxing, trying to keep my thoughts away from home. It is wooded here on both sides, and I can hear all sorts of wild animals and birds. I can easily identify the sound of the hoot owl and that of the coyote, but there are many other voices out in the night besides theirs. Just a few moments ago I checked my two anchors, and I heard a large splash from shore and a kind of grunt. It could have been an alligator. It could also have been a beaver — and, if so, I hope he has no appetite for nylon anchor lines!

It's chilly up here, and I know that it's time to go below. A cold front will move through tomorrow, and it looks as though the good daytime weather is about to be over, too. Finally, I'll admit to a bit of loneliness.

November 27 and 28
Mile 28, Arkansas River

I used yesterday for nothing more than getting to Pine Bluff, where I stocked up on enough supplies to make it to Greenville, Mississippi — I hope. Last night was spent on Lake Langhofer at Pine Bluff. The lake is an old horseshoe-shaped channel of the river, converted into its present state. All around me were numerous terminals for barge traffic carrying loads of soybeans, oil products, asphalt, and steel. I guess *White Knuckles* felt dwarfed in her surroundings.

I met the owner of this marina this morning, and, in Oklahoma terms, it turned out that he was a minor celebrity. His name is Bobby Daniels, and he's the brother-in-law of Barry Switzer, coach of the University of Oklahoma's football team — at this writing, the winningest coach in the Big Eight Conference.

In Oklahoma, college football isn't a sport, it's a religion. And Switzer is its high priest. I'm a convert like just about everybody else who lives in the Sooner State, so I spent part of this morning talking football with Barry Switzer's brother-in-law. Yup — it was a big thrill.

I made a friend, too. Mr. Daniels wound up making a trip into Pine Bluff for me to purchase some needed supplies. He's a nice fellow, and I'll never begrudge the late start I got because of my visit with him. Besides, *White Knuckles* and I made two more locks today — not to mention about twenty-seven miles. That's not a bad day on the river.

Those locks still never fail to awe me. They're an experience — no doubt about it. Once inside a lock with the gates closed and the discharge beginning to lower *White Knuckles* and me, I always feel the power of the river. It thunders and growls and presses at the upper gate, trying its best to get in, reminding me of a hungry lion. The lock gates are all that contain this hungry force, and they seem barely able to hold their own against it.

Today the cold front arrived. The wind came up out of the north at about 1530, and before long the temperature was dropping. I managed to get us into an anchorage about 100 feet out of the marked channel in about seven feet of water. That's not excellent. I've tried to guard the boat further by throwing out two bow anchors with fifty feet of line, certainly not enough for this current and wind — but, on the other hand, too much if the wind should change and set us toward shore. A tow of barges passed shortly after I had anchored and hardly disturbed the boat at all. Ironically, though, I think the wind and the current probably flattened the wake considerably — which left me with the same wind and current to worry about during the night. Clearly, it wasn't going to be an easy night.

I set the alarm every two hours and checked to see how we were lying. At 0300, I awoke to find that I could feel no wind and no current at all.

Now, that was truly terrifying. No current could have meant that we were drifting. I rushed out to the cockpit — but to my great relief, all our lights and landmarks were still in place, which meant that we were still in place. Evidently neither the dam below nor the dam above was discharging water at all, which accounted for the lack of current.

"White Knuckles," I said aloud, "we're going to make it through another night." For an answer, I got night sounds. The stars, what appeared to be a million, shined brightly down, so close it seemed that I could reach out and touch them. In that moment, I was lonely no more. It occurred to me, as it occurs to us all in such moments, that all those stars, planets, and our own small world — this garden of the universe — are all part of some great clockwork, set in

motion long ago, running for centuries upon centuries. When moments like these come, how can one feel alone? There has to be some giant will — some enormous, computer-like mind — behind all this. How else could all of it be so precise? I think that the human mind compared to the mind of whatever is out there must be rather like an orange as compared to the sun. It's all more than I can comprehend. Like many another before me, I decided, standing there on the deck beneath the stars, humbly to leave my thoughts where they were. Let God take care of the heavens. I have *White Knuckles* to take care of.

It does come down to that: I simply must do anything necessary to take care of this boat. It has, after all, taken very good care of me. My love for this boat is an unreasonable one, unshakable as a man's love for a woman, and growing each day. I would spend endless nights like this one to protect her.

November 29 and 30
Mile 583, Mississippi River

The Mississippi!

On this last day of November, *White Knuckles* and I have entered onto the Father of Waters. In some ways, everything thus far has been done with this day in mind — and we made it! If I had a bottle of champagne, I'd open it — but coffee will have to suffice. I sit tonight in the cabin, writing this, with the impression that we are still under way. On this river, there is constant motion while anchored, and there is the ceaseless sound of water rushing past. Of all the days of my life, this will be, I know, one of the most memorable. We're on the Big River.

We were wise to spend yesterday negotiating the Post Canal which connects the Arkansas River to the White River and to the Mississippi. Last night we anchored next to the canal on Lake Merrisach. It seemed as if we were not on the river at all, if truth be told — Lake Merrisach has a public-use area, maintained by the Corps of Engineers, which offers picnic tables, restrooms, and even showers. The area, like all the ones along the navigation system, is more like a city park, well-kept and clean. From the boat ramp I could see, in close proximity, several house trailers and mobile homes. I thought it strange to see so many of them at this time of the year until I realized that their owners, in turn, were probably wondering about the nut out there on the boat. I felt communal toward them, though, fancying that they, too, were traveling south — they with their wheels and I with a boat named *White Knuckles,* pilgrims all.

This glorious, bright day seemed planned just for *White Knuckles* and me — and I found myself wishing that it could last forever. We negotiated the last two locks (that's seventeen in all), a drawbridge, and the rest of the Post Canal. Then we were on the White River, our gateway to the Mississippi.

Sometime during the morning, I looked ahead at a bend in the river and saw the largest tow of barges I had ever seen, broadside. We had just left a straight stretch of river, and thinking that it would be a better location to meet this monster, I turned back toward it. But after regaining that straightaway, I maneuvered the boat around to meet the tow — which was nowhere to be seen!

Where did it go? Of course, it was on the Mississippi, and I would never meet it. In less than a mile, *White Knuckles* and I would encounter that river.

We did. When we first met the current, the boat lurched — and that little motor I have cursed so often really started to work. As Huck Finn said, "It's a monstrous big river down there" — and it surely is that. We reached midchannel and turned downstream, and our speed increased noticeably. We were smack in the middle of the mighty Mississippi.

I looked around at this mass of a river, and the boat seemed smaller to me, the motor downright tiny. In truth, the motor is tiny for this river; it will not push *White Knuckles* upstream at all. While anchoring tonight, I turned upstream and realized that while the boat was throwing a nice bow wave and the rudder was most responsive, even with the motor full out we were not moving at all. This is going to be a different ball game.

Different in quite a few other ways, too. Barge traffic here is very heavy. In only ten miles on the Mississippi today, we have already met ten large tows and have been passed by two. On the basis of my experience today, I'm still inclined to believe that some of those harrowing tales I heard about the wakes of the barges were exaggerated. We came through all of our encounters today in good shape.

Of course, we may not have seen the biggest specimens yet. The largest one today was six barges wide and about eight barges long. The tugs pushing them throw water ten feet high, but this is from their propellers. The actual wake seems to be three or four feet high, going on for about ten minutes. Later they will rebound from each shore, starting the whole thing over again — in less rough fashion. But it hasn't been bad so far.

At one point, we met two tows, one passing the other, and this was unnerving. It proved to be nothing serious, however, because the two wakes seemed to cancel each other somewhat. The water was choppy — but if choppy is as bad as it gets, we'll make it. Those tows are immense, though. At night, as I saw just a few minutes ago, they look like lighted city blocks floating along. We're stopped about 200 yards out of the buoyed channel for our first night on the Mississippi, and so we're taking the wakes of the tows on the beam tonight.

It's green down here. The willow trees have most of their green leaves still intact — and there's Spanish moss on some trees as well. We may have left the pine trees behind at Little Rock, but there are clearly going to be scenic compensations here. Southland, here we come! The big adventure is at last fully under way!

December 1 and 2
Mile 559, Mississippi River

There won't be any entry for yesterday. It was a thoroughly harrowing day, the only one of the trip thus far — and I sincerely hope the last one. If I go through another one like yesterday — I must admit it — I'm going to think seriously about turning back.

I didn't eat all day. In fact, when I was finally able to even think about eating, I was, at that point, so exhausted and disheartened that I simply fell into my bunk and slept for ten straight hours. Only today, in the clear light of morning, can I even begin to assess what happened. But now I can see how one mistake can bring on another, and how this can start a multitude of misadventures.

Yesterday morning was windless, and *White Knuckles* and I were motoring along the outside edge of the channel, enjoying the Mississippi and perhaps just a bit prideful that we had made it. At that moment, it seemed to me that the rest of our journey was going to be virtually effortless.

That's when the motor suddenly stopped.

There was not time, of course, to think of how much trouble I'd had with that contrary contraption before or of what I should have done to guard against this possibility. Within seconds, we were broadside to the current, moving swiftly downstream. The overwhelming sensation I felt was pure powerlessness.

Maybe that is why I overreacted. Whatever the reason, that was the point at which I made my first mistake. That mistake, far more than the motor outage, turned yesterday into a day of horrors.

I dropped the bow anchor. Not very wise! When it grabbed bottom, the boat changed ends so suddenly that I was nearly thrown overboard. But there was worse to come.

The anchor held, and I quickly reoriented myself enough to go to work on the motor. I finally got it started, but it was running very badly. I tried my best to power up to the anchor, but this proved impossible due to the strong current. So I raised the sail, hoping to sail and power up at the same time. But I couldn't get any slack, not the slightest bit, in the anchor line. It remained bar-taut.

And then the real trouble came.

A large tree, forked and at least forty feet long, swept down virtually out of nowhere, straddled the anchor line, and swept it under the keel. Once more, *White Knuckles* went broadside to the current. And this time, the port rail was completely buried.

The motor died again — drowned out, obviously. I fought panic and rigged another line to the anchor line, leading it back around a winch. I hoped to either winch up to the anchor or somehow dislodge that tree. But this, too, was a bad decision. The result of my action was that the port rail was only buried more and more. A numbing thought hit me — we could go under.

But I was still in the game, still playing to win. I sheeted in the sails hard and cut loose the anchor, losing it forever — along with about 100 feet of new nylon line. That, however, was the least of my worries. I was just damned glad to be rid of that tree. The port rail rose slowly. "Sorry, Girl," I breathed out loud. "I nearly finished us."

We sailed across the river to a sandy island, one which looked for all the world like some place where Huck and Jim might once have put in. But glad as I was to see it, I couldn't appreciate the literary connection. I saw it as a haven all right, though — a place to rest for a few moments and collect my scattered thoughts.

I dropped anchor — my next mistake.

The anchor wouldn't hold no matter what I did. Before I knew it we were slowly moving downstream, almost stopping occasionally, but never for long. How could this have happened? When we drew near the island, we couldn't have been in more than twenty feet of water!

We remained in this sad situation most of the day. I must have looked unbearably clownish to some presiding river god out there — I was scurrying about the deck, trying desperately to stop my own boat. With the first signs of approaching dusk, I felt the cold hand of panic clutch my heart once more. On the river at night, a prisoner of the current, I wouldn't stand much of a chance to see the morning without serious mishap.

I hoisted the distress flag. But the day had passed with surprisingly little traffic along the way, and now no one came in sight. Finally, at about 2100, after I had dragged for a steady three miles, I saw a small tow of nine barges approaching from upstream. I fired a flare.

Soon a motor launch approached from the tow, carrying two men. In the near dark, I could barely see them — but they were the most welcome sight I had yet seen on the river.

"Got trouble?" one called out as they came alongside. They appeared to be father and son, the older perhaps sixty and the younger in his thirties. They had the look of seasoned river pilots, and they obviously had rescued fledgling sailors in trouble before.

"Bum motor," I told them. "And I haven't been able to make my anchor hold." There was great relief in my voice, and I knew that the two of them could perceive that I had been badly scared. But by that point, I just didn't care.

"We'll tow you back to where that anchor will hold," the younger of my rescuers told me. "Hang on, you're all right now."

I was more than willing to take their word for it. They towed us to a backwater area where the anchor, sure enough, did hold. I looked around and found that I was surrounded by driftwood of sizes varying from branch length to power-line pole length. It all just moved slowly about in a circle, and I could see that it would not damage *White Knuckles* during the night.

"Sorry about this," I told the men.

"It's happened before," the older one said, "and it'll happen again." He stuck out a weathered hand. "I'm Bill Fitzgerald, and my friend is Herb Fleischer. Glad we could help you."

We shook hands. So they were not father and son, but captain and mate. The two relationships, I told myself, are very similar.

We agreed that they would check on me in the morning, and I bade them good-bye. I was exhausted and filled with self-doubt. I hadn't handled the situation well at all today, and I knew it. I wanted some time to myself, time to sort things out.

Later, I checked my map. All this had begun at Choctaw Bend, mile 559, between Arkansas City, Arkansas, and Greenville, Mississippi. I knew I'd never forget that place.

"Sorry, Girl," I said again, realizing that I'd spent a good part of the day apologizing — and fighting the river. I knew that I would have to make friends with it again tomorrow.

Early this morning, true to their word, Bill Fitzgerald and Herb Fleischer returned. They invited me to breakfast aboard their tug, and I gratefully accepted.

"It's catching," Bill told me as soon as we were under way. "We've got engine trouble, too. We're tied to the bank of the river about a mile downstream."

I didn't know whether to laugh — my first reaction — or to be stoically concerned. It was Herb who resolved the problem for us. "If you get yours fixed first," he deadpanned, "can we get you to tow those barges for us?"

We all had a good laugh then, and soon we were enjoying a working man's breakfast with the tug's crew of eight — including a lady cook. I practically inhaled my food, and then looked up in embarrassment.

"I'm afraid I didn't eat yesterday," I told them. "A little too much going on."

The cook — whose name was Ginny McCoy and who, at approximately fifty, was every bit as grizzled as the rest of them — laughed heartily and dished me up some more eggs and biscuits. "From what I hear," she told me, "you did about ten good days' work in just one."

"I'm afraid you're right," I told her, then launched into my second breakfast plate as if I'd never had a first one.

After our meal, I got a tour of the tug. It truly was a home on the river. This crew lived and worked on the boat for weeks at a time, so they treated it like they might treat their own domiciles. Everything was wonderfully neat and clean; for the first time, I truly understood the meaning of the word *shipshape*. When we got to the engine room, I saw that the power plant for the tug consisted of a couple of 900-horsepower diesel engines. One of them was leaking fuel.

"That's the problem," Captain Bill told me. "We've got to put in for repairs. You can't push nine barges with a leaking engine."

"What's on the barges?" I inquired.

"Rock," Bill told me. "Good, heavy Kentucky rock. Weighs about 150 tons, all told."

I whistled.

"Don't get too overcome," he laughed. "That's a small load compared with what we're used to."

Bill had already put in a radio call to his superiors, and even now another tug was on its way to pick up him and his barges that afternoon. A thought occurred to me — one that wasn't really in keeping with the spirit of my journey, but one which, I realized, might be a solution to my problems.

"What if I were to tie on?" I asked him. "We could both get the service we need at the same place, maybe."

"We'd have to beat the insurance to do something like

that," Bill told me regretfully. "And it's been my experience that nobody beats the insurance. Our policy just won't let anybody hook on."

I laughed. "Picking up hitchhikers is verboten, huh?" I kidded him.

"Afraid so," he told me. "But anything else we can do, we'll be glad to." He winked. "Sailors got to stick together," he said, and I felt somehow that I had been admitted to a secret society.

"I'd love to see the bridge," I said, and he took me up. From there, the river opened, it seemed, endlessly. I could see *White Knuckles* far below — a mile away. She looked tiny from there, and I wondered for a moment how I could ever have believed that she could weather the Mississippi. Even this tug, equipped to pull 150 tons, was in trouble. I had been presumptuous.

"I wonder if we'll make it," I said to myself, but Bill, of course, overheard.

"I don't know," Bill said. "But I've learned enough about you this morning to know that if you quit now, you'll never forgive yourself."

I turned to him and was instantly glad that it had been this fellow who picked me up last night and then invited me for this breakfast. I'd told them of my journey thus far, and of my plan to get to New Orleans — or maybe as far as I could, in my happier fantasies. Bill and his crew hadn't had the reaction I'd grown used to from my meetings with fishermen and marina owners. They hadn't said they wished they were going with me or that they envied me. They lived the river almost every day of their lives, and they knew the chances that *White Knuckles* and I were taking. They weren't opposed to my plans, but they were clear eyed about them. That was why I had so much respect for what Bill had just said.

I shook his hand, and we looked at each other warmly. "You're right," I told him. "Thanks."

Herb took me back to *White Knuckles* just before noon. I knew I'd be sailing for Greenville tomorrow, but I certainly wasn't going to try it today. I was bone weary. I had to learn how to deal with this awesome river, and I had to do so quickly.

Bill and Herb had given me plenty of pointers throughout the morning. On the way back to *White Knuckles,* Herb explained how to find "slack" water to anchor in, and Bill had explained many of the river's characteristics to me. But I wasn't feeling very happy. Before, I had been confident out of ignorance. Now, with new knowledge, I found myself subdued and downright apprehensive.

That afternoon I cleaned the boat and tried to put everything in order for tomorrow's sail. This would be the first time I'd be forced to depend on the skill I thought I'd learned back on Lake Hefner during long and happy weekends last summer. Now we'd see how well I had learned.

Partway through my cleanup, I discovered that *White Knuckles* had circled several times during the night and this morning. The anchor line was wrapped around her fin keel and around the rudder. How in God's name was I to free it? My first worry, though, was that now I wouldn't even have enough line to drop anchor since the line was so tangled — so I inflated the dinghy. I was going to row ashore with about 200 feet of line and tie the boat to a tree, so paranoid had I become about coming unanchored.

Two fishermen came alongside at that point. After I explained the problem, they offered to carry the line over for me. They told me Greenville was the nearest place to get the motor worked on. Both of them agreed that my precautions in tying up the boat are in keeping with my surroundings which, as it turns out, are incredibly isolated. If I get into trouble during the night I'll definitely be on my own.

The fishermen went on their way with my line, and I stayed on the deck, watching the sunset. As I stood there, I watched the sister tug to Bill's take my new friends on their way. We waved to each other; Bill and Herb were clearly visible on the bridge. I'm hoping to see them downriver. I miss them already.

I have learned a lot during these past two days, and I've learned it at some cost. Probably my best lesson has been never to anchor in the main current. Three strong men couldn't have pulled up to the anchor I dropped yesterday. That first night I anchored in the main current must have been a fluke — pure luck. Otherwise, I never could have gotten out of there the next morning. I also know now to sail far above any intended anchoring or landfall, and I know that I could have saved myself a great deal of trouble by doing so yesterday when I made for the island. It was at least a mile downstream, and we still barely made it before being swept past. That was in a light wind, too!

Now what am I to do about my tangled line? Attach a

smaller line to the bitter end, let it slack off, and see if it will sink away from around the keel? If the motor were working, I could try spinning the boat — but which way? The fishermen had offered no advice, and I had to admit that I was fresh out of ideas, too.

Perhaps a good night's sleep will provide the solution. This is the longest entry in my log so far and with good reason — it's been the longest two days I can remember.

December 3 and 4
Mile 552, Mississippi River

We made just seven miles yesterday; a light wind and a bum motor held us back. The problems I had envisioned in getting the anchor up, however, did not materialize. I awoke yesterday morning to find part of the anchor line floating on the water at the stern. I simply cleated it fast, untied the bitter end at the bow, and worked it out from around the rudder and keel, stern-side. But the heavy traffic on the Mississippi is going to take some getting used to — *White Knuckles* is surrounded by driftwood at night because of the constant water turmoil that the endless barge movement generates. I can see now why the railroads fought the inland-waterways system so bitterly. It's quite common to see forty barge tows in a day on this river, some of them with up to fifty barges each.

But today, quite early in the morning, I hitched a ride into Dermott, Arkansas — having missed Arkansas City yesterday — with *White Knuckles's* little motor under my arm. Then I returned to the landing where we had put in the night before and found a ruddy-cheeked fellow about my age awaiting me. I'd met him only briefly the night before. His name, I knew, was Wells — and he and his wife owned this landing.

"Find the shop all right?" he asked me. He'd given me the name of a small-motor repair place the previous evening.

"I did," I told him. "And thanks. It should be ready later today."

"In that case," he said, "you've got lots of time to join my missus and me for a lunch."

I was still bone tired and not really in the mood for my usual noon fare of cheese and crackers. "Mr. Wells," I told him, "I don't mind if I do."

I ate my first home-cooked meal since I dined with my friends in Little Rock, and it was a lovely table that Arline Wells set. She was a sort of female counterpart to Bobby, with the same ruddy cheeks and quick humor. Over an excellent meat loaf, the two of them told me all about how they came to own this landing and what they planned to do with it. Bobby was in the process of enlarging and improving it — and he had good credentials for such work because he was a contractor by trade. I observed that the two of them must have saved for a long time to put together the investment that this work was surely costing.

Bobby laughed. "Wasn't so long ago that I was flat broke," he said, and even his red cheeks seemed to turn a little pale at the memory. "Compliments of the Corps of

Engineers. Damn near lost everything."

"Sounds rough," I observed. Bobby seemed anxious to tell the story.

"Rough ain't the word," he told me. "I'd contracted to drive some pilings for the corps, and it looked like an easy job. But the site turned out to be solid rock beneath the surface, and that caused the job to take twice as long as I thought it would. But a contract's a contract where I come from, so I forged ahead."

"So what went wrong?" I asked.

Bobby pushed back his plate. "Everything," he told me, "when nothing should have. I had a clause in the contract which stated that there would be extra pay for such unforeseen obstacles, and I figured I was covered."

"But the corps didn't," I said, anticipating where this was going.

"You got it," he said. "They refused to pay once the job was finished. Oh, they paid the original fee, all right — but everything extra was on me. And the extra came to $500,000."

I whistled.

"Damn right," he said with conviction. "And we're still in appeal. The damn litigation has already cost me my equipment and Arline and me a home." He reached across the table and took his wife's hand. "Everything we had left is in this landing," he finished.

"How are your chances to win the case?" I asked.

"They're good," Arline put in, "if you really believe that the bureaucrats can be beat. I can't tell you how many hours we've spent — wasted — chasing faceless and nameless government people who were supposed to help us. But once you get through all the red tape, there's an end in sight."

I couldn't help but wonder if anybody ever really did get through all of it, but I didn't say so. Bobby and Arline saw themselves as rugged individualists up against a giant bureaucracy, and I've always had a soft spot for such folks. "I hope you win," I told them.

Over coffee, Bobby gave me some information about the stretch of river I'd just survived. According to him, the section from the mouth of the White River to Greenville is the fastest and deepest part of the river. There's an eleven-foot drop back there in a very few miles, all in an extremely narrow channel. And I was through that. The thought cheered me.

"On past Vicksburg," Bobby told me, "the river slows and widens. But the current is faster. What does that little motor of yours do?"

"Six miles per hour," I told him.

"You need one that does seven or eight," he said. "That's what the current is going to be. Put in at Greenville tomorrow and see if there's anything bigger to be had. Take my word."

Thinking I could probably do worse than rely on the word of a fellow who would take on the Corps of Engineers, I promised that I would look into another motor and stood up to bid my new friends a good afternoon.

"Bobby and I would love to have you stay here tonight," Arline told me. "As you can see, we're still finishing the house, but there's plenty of room."

"I'm pretty used to sleeping on the boat," I told her.

"It'll just make you appreciate a real bed more," she said. "Come on back up for supper."

Just like that, she talked me into it. A couple of more encounters like this one, and I'm in danger of becoming a landlubber again.

DECEMBER 5
Greenville Harbor on Lake Ferguson
(Greenville, Mississippi)

Twenty days until Christmas! This morning, Arline Wells drove me into town to pick up my motor. It had taken the full day to fix it, after all. Along the way, she taught me some local history.

"Dermott is where the first railroad in Arkansas was started," she told me. "And the first railroad station there was called the Bowie Station."

"After Jim Bowie?" I asked.

"Close," she told me. "After his brother, in fact — John Bowie, who was called 'Old Bowie.' He was one of our earliest settlers."

"A settler is always a safe bet for naming things after," I joked.

"Better than that," Arline told me, "he was also one of the first businessmen in the area. A 'founding father,' I believe the term is. And we've got some more items of interest, too. There's a landing not far away called Gaines Landing. It was the old stagecoach stop, years ago, which picked up river travelers and took them to Washington, Arkansas."

"And why would they want to go there?" I asked her.

"Because Washington used to be the capital of the state!" she informed me. "All this took place in just two large counties — Desha and Chicot. To this day, they're larger than some of the New England states. And they say Texas is big!" she laughed. "We've got all this and the Mississippi, too."

After we picked up the motor, Arline drove me back to *White Knuckles*. We'd anchored this time not too far from an old barge, and I was anxious to get away from that decrepit thing before it disintegrated.

Nonetheless, the hospitality of the Wellses had been wonderful, and I was very sad to bid farewell to these two good friends. Once again, I'd been reminded that I too had a marriage — one that I had forsaken for this journey, for *White Knuckles*.

"May the wind be at your back," Bobby told me. He'd taken time from restoring his landing to come down and see us off. He and Arline stood now with arms linked.

"Thanks, you two," I said. "Thanks for everything." And *White Knuckles* and I cast off. There was a bit of a lump in my throat, the same loneliness I'd felt when I said good-bye to Howard and Betty Wills. Why did these visits to homes of people permanently committed to one another always seem to depress me so?

But the depression was gone after an hour or so on the

river. We sailed into Greenville in the late afternoon under full main and lapper. The river had been swift all day and the wind hard against the current, creating a rather vicious chop. It was the roughest sailing I had ever done — and also the most invigorating. One rail or the other on this boat was buried in water all the way, and the sails were wet halfway up the mast. If we hadn't had the right direction and force of wind to set us into Greenville Harbor, we could have been in trouble. It was a relief finally to sail onto the placid waters of Lake Ferguson. Sailing the five miles across the lake to the marina was like being back on Lake Hefner again.

Before turning in tonight, I talked with a Coast Guard man who had been back up the river taking depth soundings. He told me an unnerving story — about the old barge I'd been anchored next to so recently. It broke its aft mooring cable and swung around. It's now lying where *White Knuckles* rested not twenty-four hours ago. Is this, I wonder, a sign that somebody up there likes us . . . or is it a warning?

December 6 and 7
Mile 500, Mississippi River

We need to make Vicksburg tomorrow. The radio reports a strong cold front moving in within two days, and I don't want us caught between cities. It's just too cold on the river at night — cold, lonely, and dangerous.

We spent yesterday at Greenville, a very pretty city whose downtown section fronts the lake. I bought a new anchor and line and tried to find a larger motor, but *White Knuckles* requires a model with a long shaft — there were none of those to be had. But I got the supplies I needed and did some laundry. The people of Greenville seem full of southern hospitality; almost everyone I met on the sidewalk smiled and spoke. I'd been afraid I was starting to look like the Ancient Mariner, but apparently I'm not that forbidding yet.

I spent the rest of the day wandering around the marina, talking to a surprisingly wide variety of tugboat captains, deckhands, and sailors. They were full of river stories and river background, most of it vital information. They had some background on the political forces at work on the river, too.

The old enemy of Bobby Wells, the Corps of Engineers, had adversaries among the men I talked with, too. For years, the corps has been in the apparently never-ending process of "straightening" the river, using dikes, levees, revetments, draglines, and dredges to accomplish the purpose. All this activity has caused the current of the river to increase and the channel to get deeper. Yellowbend, for example — the stretch I had just come through — is now over eighty feet deep with a current of eight miles per hour, thanks to the corps.

The upshot of all this, according to one captain I talked to, is that each year it is getting a little harder to go upstream with a tow of barges — and although it is conversely easier to go downstream, it is also a good deal trickier.

"The corps!" one old-timer told me with words tinged with contempt. "Those boys are all-powerful — or at least they think they are. But it ain't up to man to change the river. The river changes itself."

"But hasn't this work produced some good things, too?" I asked him. I reminded him, for example, that Lake Ferguson itself used to be the actual river. Now, through diking and dredging, it has become a beautiful fifteen-mile-long lake with a lot of new industry lining its east side.

The old-timer spat. "New industry," he said. "Shit."

Well, you can't please everybody. And I suppose that the Greenville of today is very different from what those who have been around for awhile remember. The city now has an outlet to the river and the gulf. There are new barge-building concerns, enormous grain elevators, and tugboat services here. It's not the place it was.

"Doesn't Old Man River ever rebel?" I asked my crotchety companion.

"Hell, yes, it does," he replied as if my question had given him some new lease on life. "Every now an' then this river will flood all over every man-made thing for miles. Y'oughta see that sight, boy. Keep ya humble."

I assured him that the river had done nothing but humble me since the moment I set sail, and I continued my walk around the marina. I learned that I had just missed a sailboat from France which spent two nights here, crewed by three Frenchmen and an Englishman. It had sailed all the way from England and then up the Saint Lawrence River to Chicago. From there it came down the Illinois and Mississippi rivers. From here it goes on down to the Panama Canal and, ultimately, to the South Pacific. I wonder if I will catch those sailors. Perhaps my delusions of grandeur are returning.

The weather looked fine this morning — no cold front yet — so *White Knuckles* and I hoisted full main and lapper and set out for Vicksburg. We finally dropped anchor at 1430; the wind had died. That in itself was surprising, since it had been against us all day. We managed to make thirty-five miles in about four-and-a-half hours. God! It feels good to be sailing this boat!

Today we passed many sandy islands which were covered with small, stunted pines and cedars. Although the land looks rather abused by nature, the river is much quieter and smoother down here — far more tranquil than it has been since I entered it. Some sailors at Greenville told me that we unwittingly had been riding a ten-foot rise that came down from the upper part of the river above St. Louis. The old-timers judged that phenomenon most unusual for this time of year, but they also told me that the crest of this flood is now ahead of me, on down the river.

And sure enough, I can see that the river is now dropping slowly.

We can't make Vicksburg tomorrow. It's sixty-five miles away, and we're just not traveling that quickly. This means another night on the river for us — and possibly the cold front on our heels will catch up. It could be a lonely, chilling river tomorrow night! But tonight, *White Knuckles* and I have found slack water behind a point of land which gives good protection from barge traffic, and we're feeling quite safe.

DECEMBER 8
Vicksburg Harbor
(Vicksburg, Mississippi)

Charles S. McAlpine of the Tennessee Volunteers. I wonder if he could have been my ancestor?

I am writing part of my entry today from his gravesite in the Vicksburg Military Cemetery. Yes, we made it to Vicksburg — all sixty-five miles. I weighed anchor at 0730 this morning with a brisk, cold north wind behind us, and we ran and reached most of the way. There was a stretch in which the river took a sharp, narrow bend to the north, and the chop was very bad. It took about an hour to negotiate a relatively short distance there, but from that point on it was smooth sailing — literally — with *White Knuckles* bounding along as if she'd finally come completely into her own. We tied up at Vicksburg at 1500.

Now I am here in this graveyard, where both rebels and Yankees are buried. It, like all of Vicksburg, is a visit to the past. Wherever one goes in this city, it is impossible to forget this country's Civil War.

I'd visited Vicksburg before, by automobile. But perhaps the very way I came here this time — my approach from the river — has made me understand how much history is here. This was, of course, the stage for one of the most vicious battles of the war, and I can now see why the struggle for this city took so long and cost so many lives. It's very hilly here, with thick underbrush, ideal for defensive fighting. Some of the old trenches can still be seen, with the opposing ones only yards away in many places. Some of the old houses here still have cannonballs embedded in their walls. One huge gun that commanded the river from a high bluff is still very much in place, its barrel warped from the heat of constant firing during the battle.

The North took the city, ultimately — but the southern soldiers and civilians held out here until starvation faced them all. In this graveyard, there are nearly complete records of all the soldiers — on either side — who are buried in here. I asked a clerk if there were any here with my surname, and thus I came to visit the grave of Charles McAlpine. I can feel the fingers of the past on my spine.

Anyone would, though, even without looking at a tombstone that bears one's name. Vicksburg, like San Francisco, is composed of very steep hills, streets, and sidewalks — but there any similarity between the two cities ends. The architecture is old southern, beautifully preserved. Even the port — on the Yazoo River which joins the Mississippi here — is dilapidated and archaic, nothing like the busy one at Greenville. Everything about Vicksburg asks you to take a step into the past.

The president of the Confederacy himself, Jefferson Davis, lived a mere fifteen miles from here on his plantation. He owned 15,000 acres, but he died a pauper, having given all his worldly goods to the Confederate cause. He was a dreamer like I am, and I feel a certain kinship. But enough of graveyards and lost causes! Tomorrow we make for Natchez!

December 9
Mile 402, Mississippi River

White Knuckles may never forgive me for the way I decked her out today. She spent most of our sailing hours looking like a floating laundry. But the weather has stayed quite nice, and I had to take advantage of the wonderful sunshine today by hanging everything out to dry — even dirty clothes. We must have been a sight!

We're thirty-nine miles from Natchez tonight, relaxing at the end of a warm, sparkling day of sailing — a Sunday, at that — with a calm river and winds that never got much more than light. It has been, in all, the quietest and most peaceful day we have spent on the river.

Once, when the wind had absolutely stopped, I just let the boat drift to see if I could control it that way — and to my surprise I could. It requires constant attention and concentration, but so does all sailing. To drift successfully, one must keep the stern to the current and not let it get very far off either way. The rudder will respond, though very slowly. I tried this for about two hours today and was able to stay within the buoyed channel at all times.

The countryside seemed to flow by, and even our meetings with barge tows went well. We passed several large ones, looking as if they might be carrying missile parts — a jarring reminder of modern life on this bucolic river. But I learned today that we can take the wake of those monsters much better when we're sailing. With sails up, sheeted in hard, *White Knuckles* does not roll nearly so much, and some of the pitch is eliminated, too. The sails seem to dampen a lot of the wild motion we're used to getting with the motor.

It was a strange day in another way, too. Part of the time we were entirely in Louisiana and at other times somewhere between Louisiana and Mississippi. Our chart showed the state line as simply "indefinite" in places where the river has taken a notion to change its course. This strange "statelessness" provided a feeling of disorientation, which was only increased by the constant sight of huge islands on all sides. These islands are only numbers on our chart, but they are so big that they must be home to somebody. They've got to have names, at least for the local people.

We're anchored near one of these nameless islands tonight, although I couldn't get entirely out of the current. But it isn't a strong one, and I'll be able to pull up the anchor. We're in six feet of water with a sandy bottom — but after the first anchor set, I dropped the second one straight down at the bow, with the line's bitter end cleated fast. My memory of anchor problems is all too recent, and the insurance of that second anchor helps me to sleep much better.

I said earlier that I'd seen Spanish moss on the trees. I haven't. People I meet keep assuring me that the first Spanish moss I see will be at Natchez. So be it. Things are getting greener all the time down here, and that makes me feel mentally warmer. We haven't beaten winter yet — but we've got a shot at it, for sure.

December 10 through 13
Mile 362, Mississippi River
(Natchez, Mississippi)

Natchez — I've got a matchbook cover I picked up tonight which reads, "The ghosts of thieves, cutthroats, ladies of the night, and riverboat gamblers dwell here eternally."

I believe it.

White Knuckles and I have moored for the past three days at a place which, in the days of the stern-wheel steamboats, was the wild, lawless, sinful part of Natchez. It's right on the riverfront, and it's separated from the "proper" part of Natchez by a high bluff.

It's called "Under the Hill."

The city fathers are trying to restore it, but I doubt that they'll rebuild those houses that Under the Hill was most famous for — its brothels. And though they may recreate the architecture, this part of town will never be the wide-open city that it once was, where killings were an everyday (and sometimes hourly) occurrence with the victims, as often as not, dumped in the river. Crime was rampant here in the nineteenth century, and this area of town had its own crude laws to live by and to die by. You entered Under the Hill at your own risk.

Some of the old buildings, of course, are standing now — with many of their original signs quite legible. Thus, legends like *Bath 15 Cents, Painless Dentist, Whiskey,* or *Girls Wanted* can still be made out. This is the oldest town on the Mississippi River, and these signs go back a long way.

We arrived here in midafternoon three days ago, after beating in light airs for thirty-nine miles. It was an easy journey, made quite pleasurable by yet another day of good weather. The cold front I had dreaded never really came in. The marina where we're anchored is built on several old barges, all tied together and anchored in deep water, connected to the shore by a catwalk. Now, *White Knuckles* and I don't really like being this close to barges, but there wasn't much choice. Shortly after we arrived, I "stepped off" one of these barges to see how big it actually was — and my paces from one side to the other told the story. The barges are about eighty-five feet wide and, from my similar measurements in the other direction, about three hundred feet long. I instantly had even more respect for what we'd been meeting on the river!

I spent my first morning in the harbor boat-cleaning, body-cleaning, and generally tidying up. Although, as I indicated, *White Knuckles* had looked like a laundry boat as we fluttered and flapped part of our way to Natchez, there was plenty of other cleaning up to be done.

By afternoon, though, *White Knuckles* and I felt as good as new — whether we were or not — and I took to the shore for a look at the proper part of Natchez. It's quite a contrast to Vicksburg. There are plenty of antebellum homes and other buildings here, too. Even though some have been carefully preserved, others are going quickly to ruin. The homes which have been placed on the National Historic Preservation list look good, and here you can get an idea of what *prosperous* meant in the heyday of King Cotton. As in Vicksburg, the people here are easygoing and most courteous.

Around the marina, I learned that the sailboat from France had left here only the day before I arrived. I'm gaining on them! In the meantime, I've made some new friends who own another sailboat, one which docked near *White Knuckles* late this afternoon. It's a beauty of a French-built boat, powered by an eighteen-horsepower engine, but definitely built for racing other sailboats. It's thirty feet in length, with an eight-foot beam. Its owners have turned out to be a father-son team from Minnesota.

Dick Sherman has sailed, by this point, from the northern part of the country to the South, chasing a dream quite similar to my own. The difference is that he has brought along his nineteen-year-old son, Richard Jr. They are a beguiling pair of Yankees in a Confederate world, and I took to them immediately. Though bigger and huskier than his rather diminutive father, the younger Richard has been called "Junior" since his birth, and that is the name he seems stuck with for life — or at least for the duration of this trip.

By the end of our first afternoon of river talk, the three of us had become such fast friends that we agreed to make the trek up the cliff to visit a club in Natchez called Bo Jangles.

"I have a college buddy," Junior reported, "who says you'll have the time of your life in there."

"How wild an evening are you looking for, Richard?" I asked him, still not able to bring myself to call him

"Junior." "I don't much want to climb that cliff just to get poured down it later."

Junior laughed. "Dad and I don't drink," he informed me. "Nobody in our family does. But we still love to go clubbing. We get off on the atmosphere."

So here I was, hooked up with a couple of teetotalers — in Natchez, of all places. I found the irony delightful and said so.

"You should have seen us in Vegas," the elder Sherman told me. "We don't gamble, either."

So we went into Natchez and had a wonderful time at Bo Jangles, even though nobody but me had a drink. I had only one, which turned out to be a darned good thing. Bright and early the next morning I in *White Knuckles* and the Shermans in their boat were awakened by shouts and commotion. Outside, a fellow who looked like he'd hoisted quite a few the night before was desperately trying to dock the biggest private yacht I'd ever seen outside a movie theatre.

"Gimme a hand, since you're up?" the newcomer asked plaintively — and we did. An hour later, which would still have been before nine, he had his power plant and tape player going full blast, ready to begin the day with a party. Can that guy be content? I asked myself. He's got to be too busy running all his gadgets.

But obviously, he was also rich. That yacht of his took on one hundred gallons of gas, seventy gallons of water, and God knows what else. It takes some money to keep a rig that size running. So, like the paupers we were, the Shermans and I retired to their boat to contemplate these matters briefly — and other more important ones, like the trip ahead of us, at much greater length.

The sailboat that the Shermans call home is named *Gamine.* That's French for *Little Girl* — and they'd like to be sailing her more, but have been forced to run with the motor because of mast problems. Dick brewed a pot of coffee, and we settled down to talk over our plans.

"We're headed the same direction," Dick announced. "Baton Rouge is the next stop. Why don't we travel together?"

"I'm sailing," I told him. "You two would run off and leave me with your motor." I actually would have welcomed the company, but I didn't want to slow them down.

Dick looked at his son. "Junior?" he inquired. "Have we got any particular place to be?"

"Not that I know of, Dad," the younger Sherman replied.

"Any special time to be there?"

"Not so far as I can recollect."

Dick Sherman put his palms on the table in front of him with an air of satisfied finality. "Then it's decided," he said. "We'll travel together."

I agreed and thanked them, indicating that if I slowed them down I wanted to be the first to know. But we had no sooner made plans to leave for Baton Rouge early in the morning than the first splatters of rain hit *Gamine's* roof above us. Though the day had been muggy with some cloud cover, this was unexpected. We consulted the radio for weather news and learned that it could rain for the rest of the afternoon.

"Let's see how it goes," I told them. "We'll keep hoping to leave in the morning. And that means I've got plenty of work to do aboard *White Knuckles* this afternoon."

Dick assured me once more that he and his son were bound by no schedule, and I departed. We agreed that tonight, on what we assumed would be our last night in Natchez, we would all three visit an authentic Under the Hill bar, and I told them I'd see them in the early evening.

I dashed back to *White Knuckles* with the rain beating a steady tattoo around me. Just before I reached her deck, I nearly collided with an old sailor, swathed in a yellow rain slicker, who was heading up to the marina.

"Think this'll last awhile?" I asked him.

"Sonny," he replied, "it's gonna be wet again tomorrow — and it's gonna be damn cold, too."

My heart sank. "How cold?" I asked him, thinking that the front that had chased us days before was now upon us at last.

"At least fifty," he told me.

I nearly laughed out loud. Fifty! "I'm from Oklahoma," I said. "It's got to get a lot below that to be cold weather to me."

"Things are different down here," he said mysteriously and went on his way. I jumped onto *White Knuckles's* deck and went below. I wasn't about to be afraid of a cold spell of fifty degrees, but the rain did bother me. I knew that a true sailor wouldn't have let it affect him, but, perhaps more than anything connected with weather, lightning is fearsome to me when I'm sailing. *White Knuckles,* after all, has a metal mast.

Dick and Junior and I ate our dinner that night in an historic Under-the-Hill bar called The Compson House. The original back bar and tables were still in use, and ancient pictures of Natchez in its pride adorned the walls. Models of the old steamboats hung from the ceiling — and behind the bar, a portrait of Samuel L. Clemens, Mr. Mark Twain himself, peered out reproachfully at us. I thought of the later Twain I had read — the dark, sad Twain of *The Mysterious Stranger* as opposed to the younger, sunnier Twain of *Tom Sawyer,* and I remembered that he had finally become so contemptuous of his fellow man that he had labeled us "the damned human race." I wondered if he had done part of his field research into human nature in the saloons of Under the Hill.

The rain pounded us all the way back to our boats, and it was with an air of wistfulness that we consulted our charts before packing it in for the night. It rained throughout the night, and by midmorning today there has still been no letup. We're landlocked!

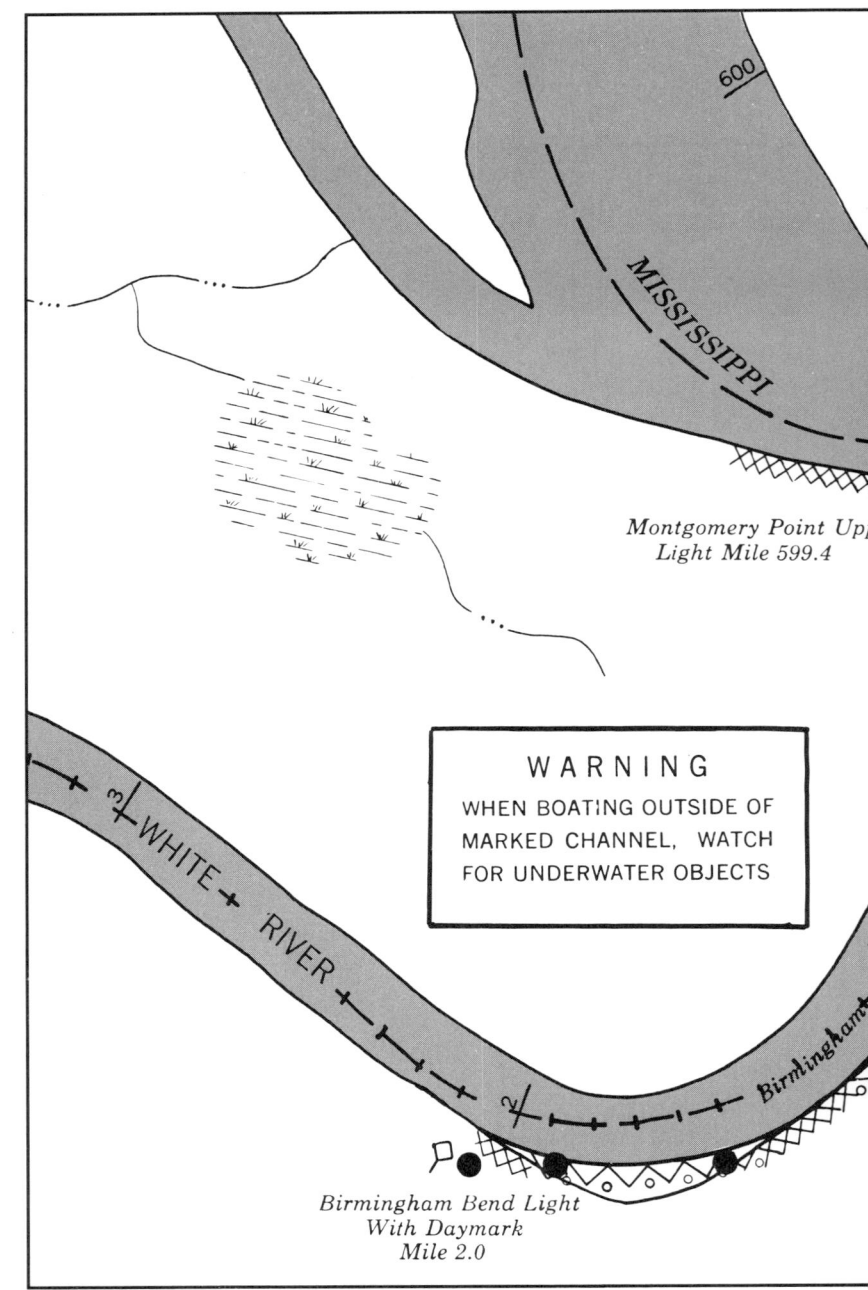

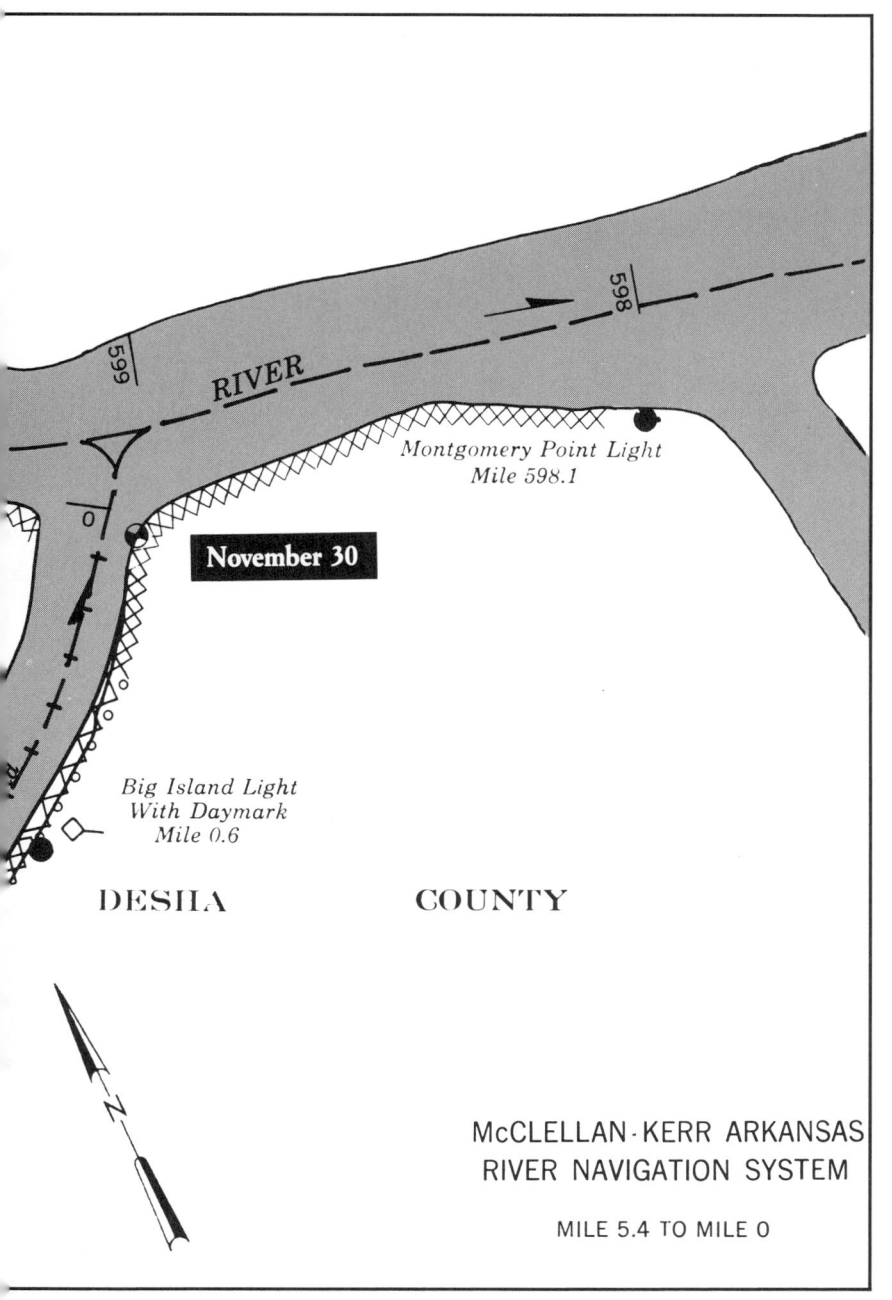

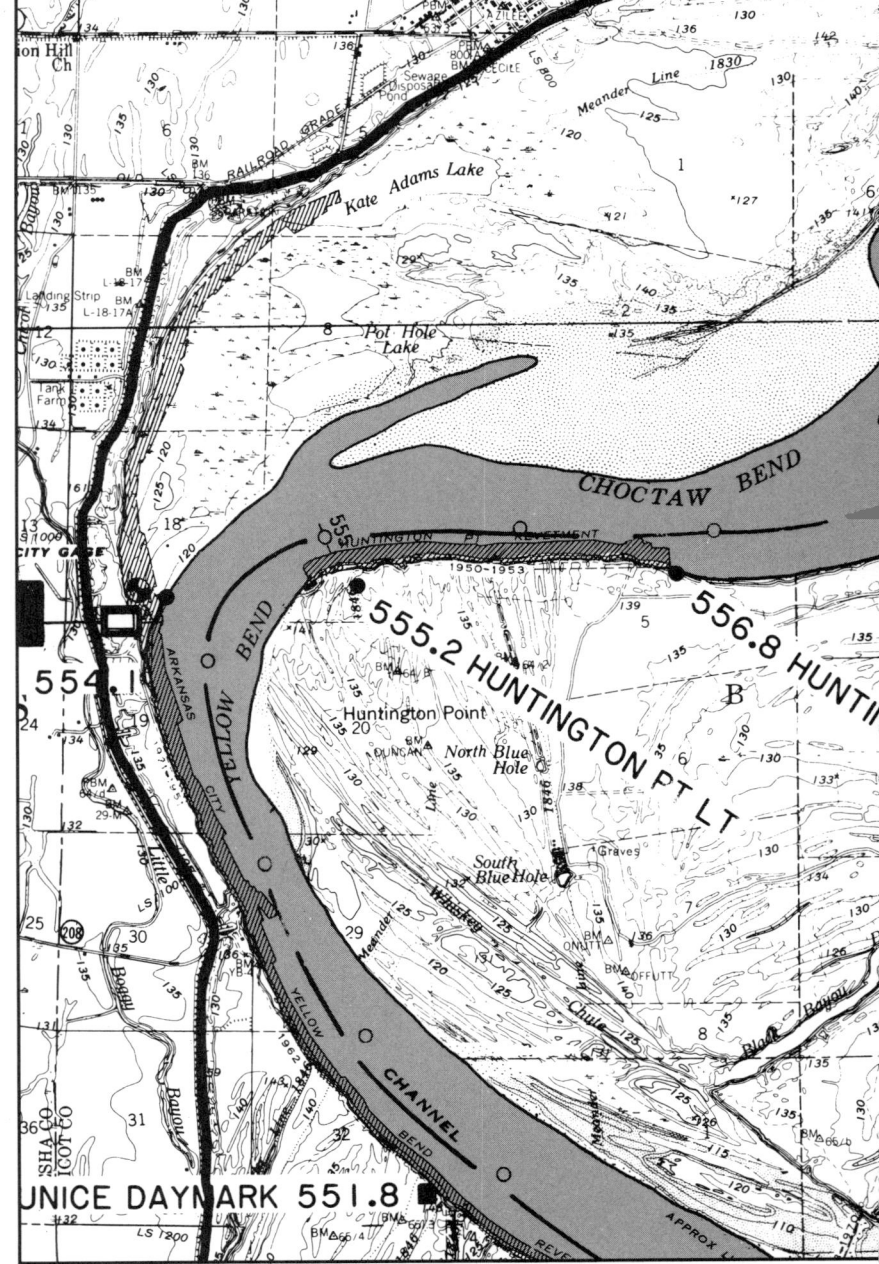

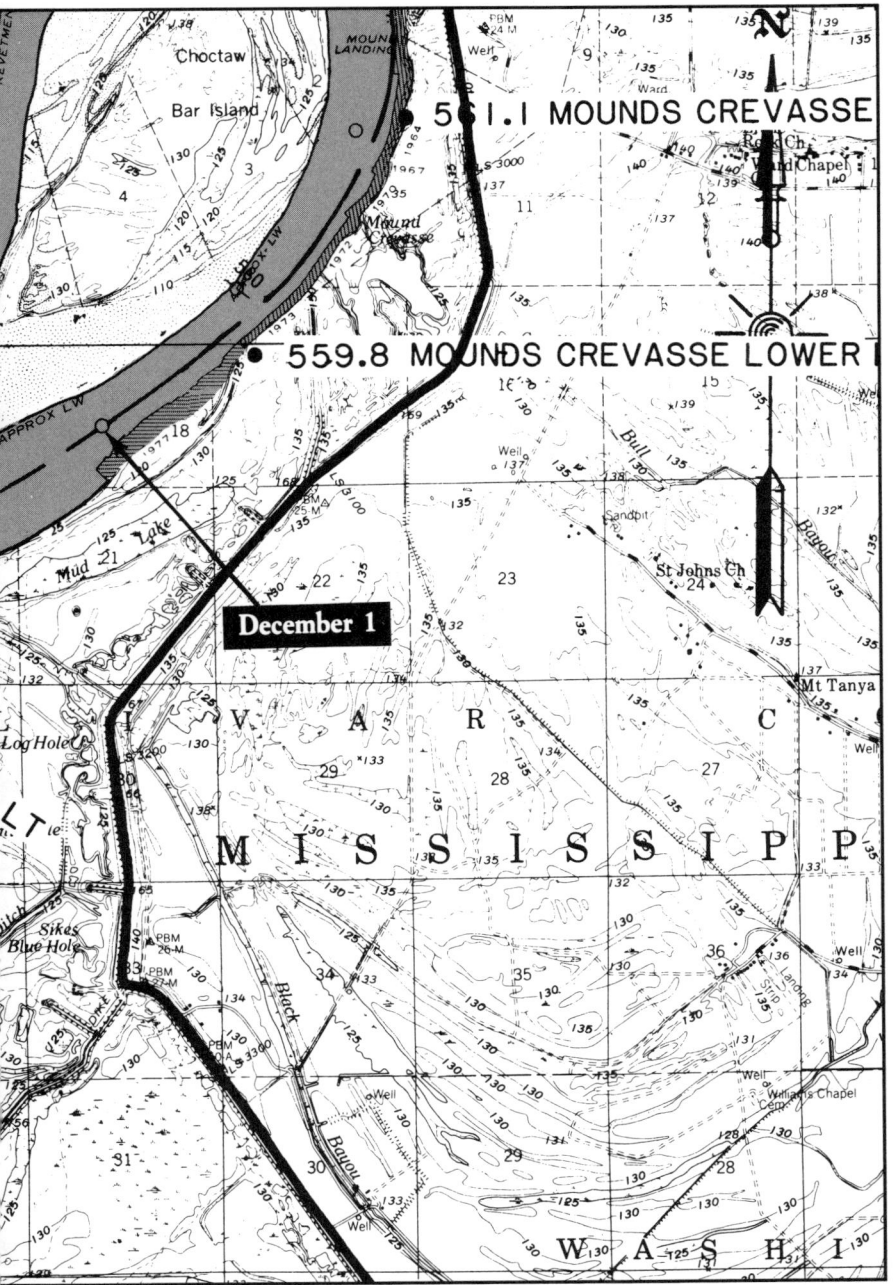

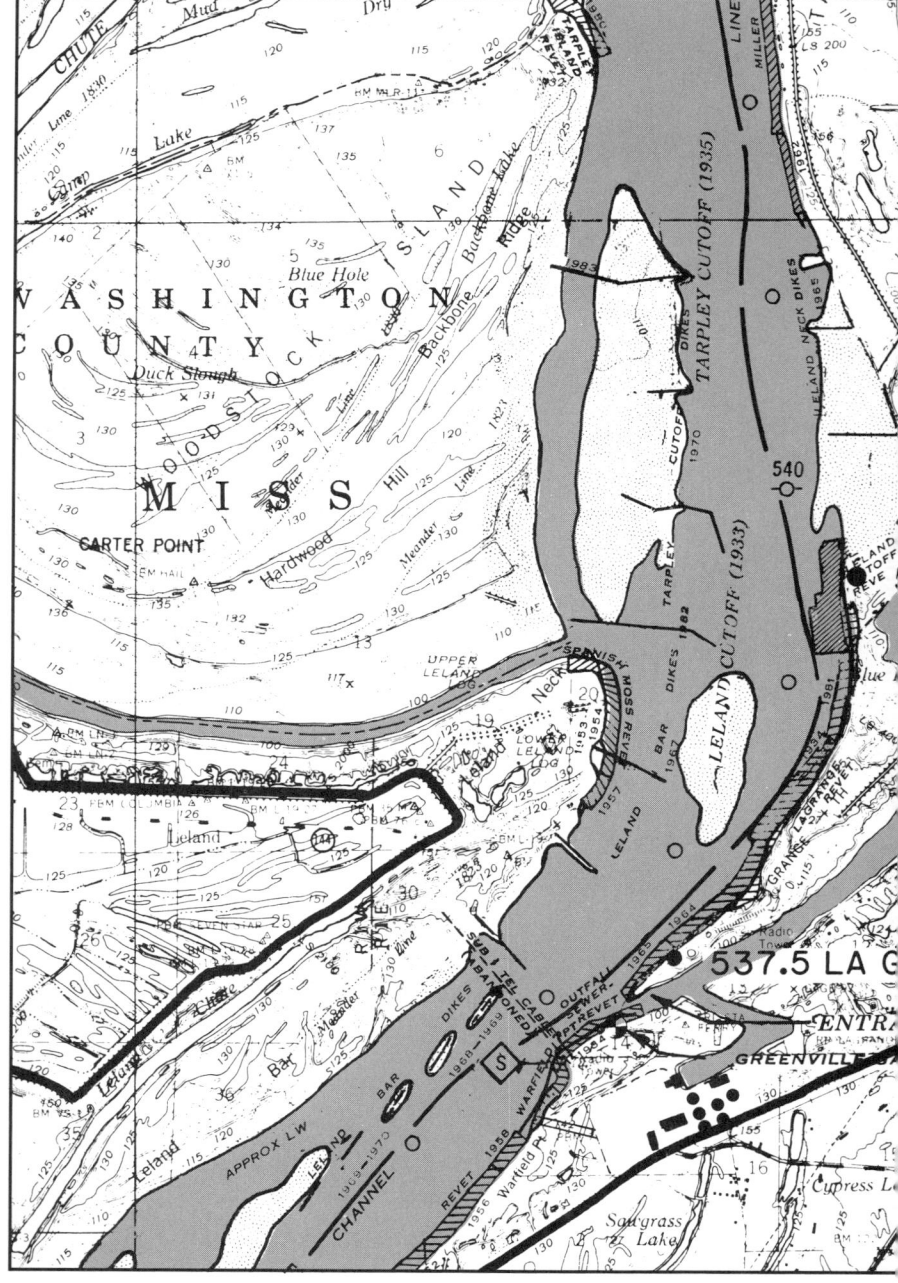

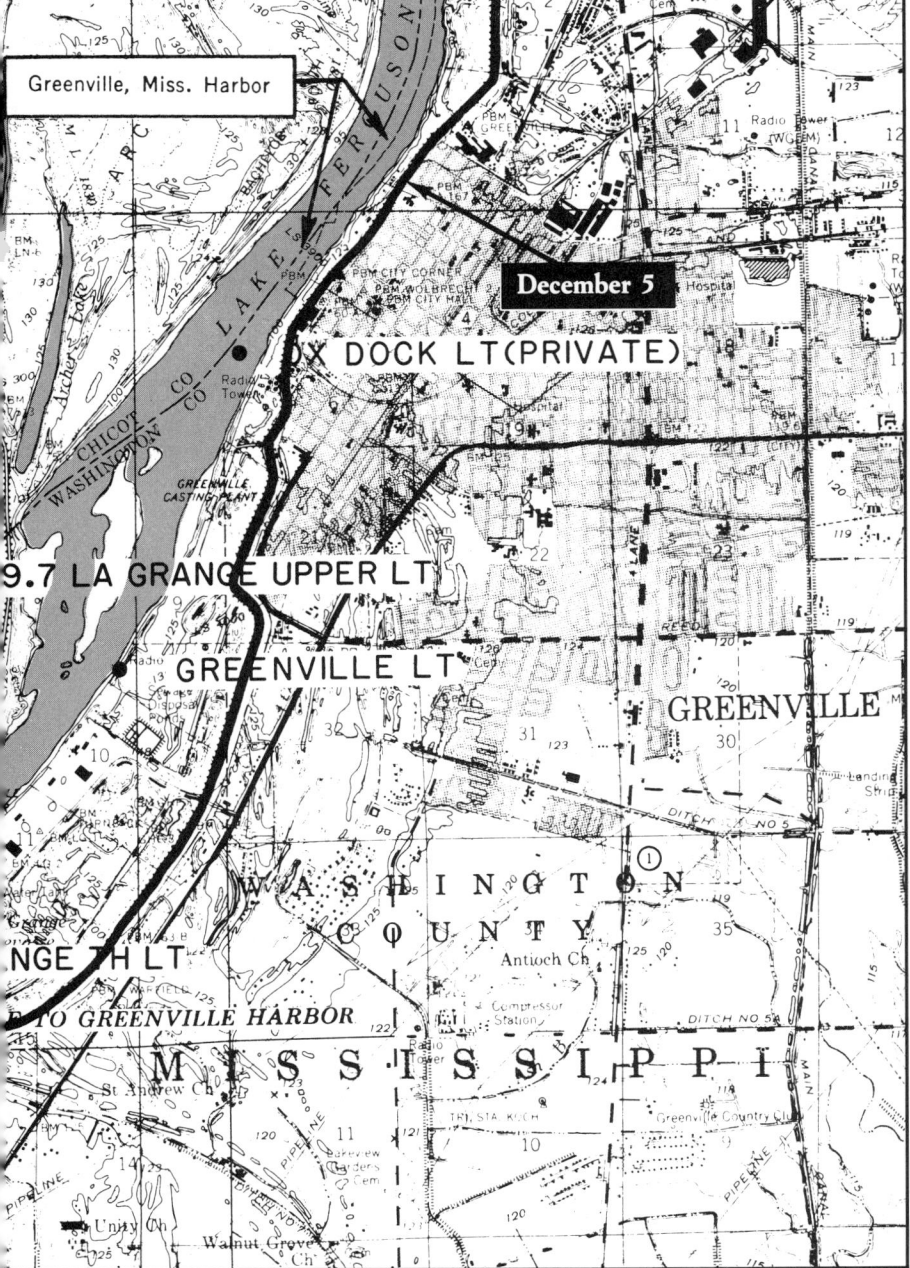

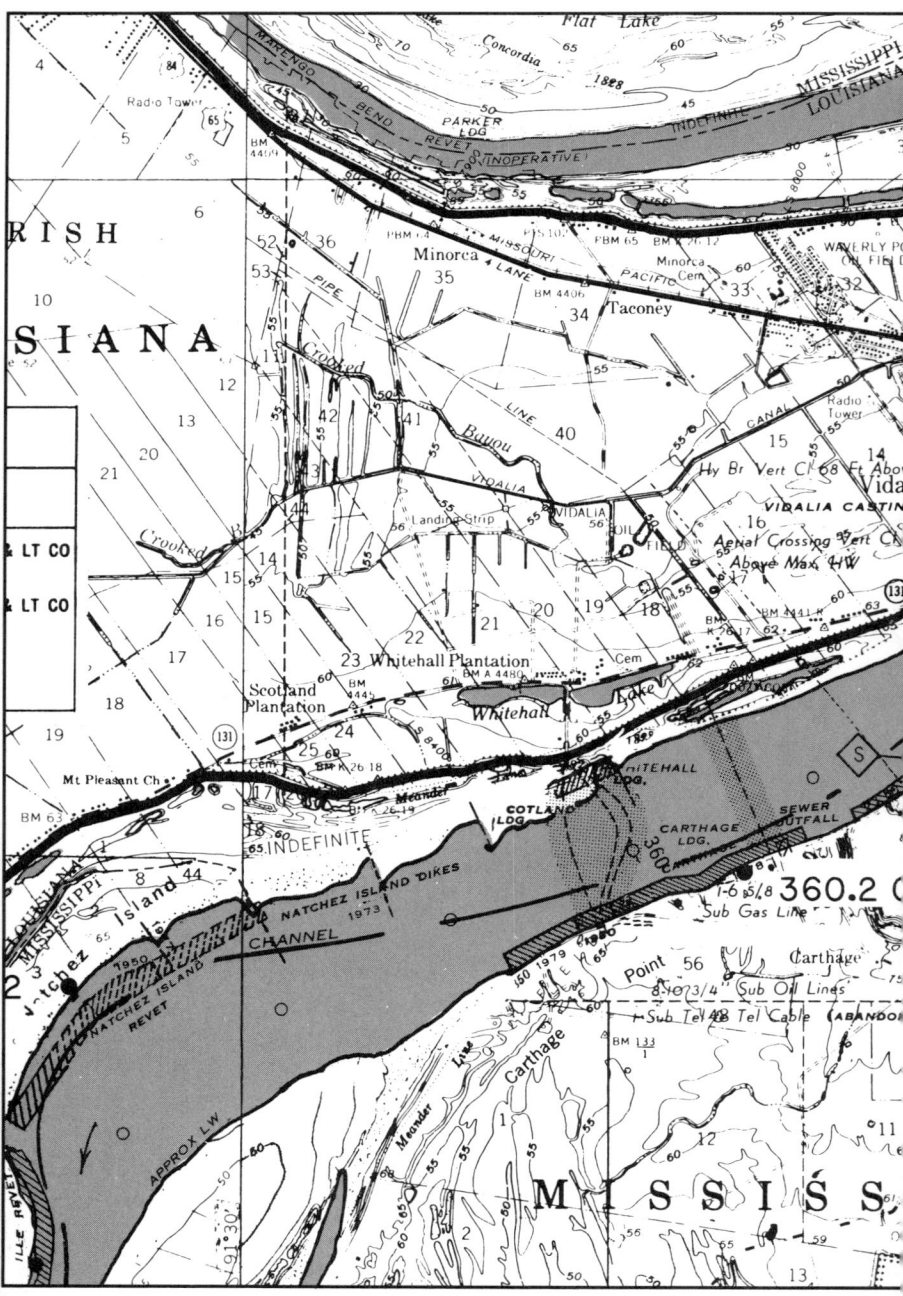

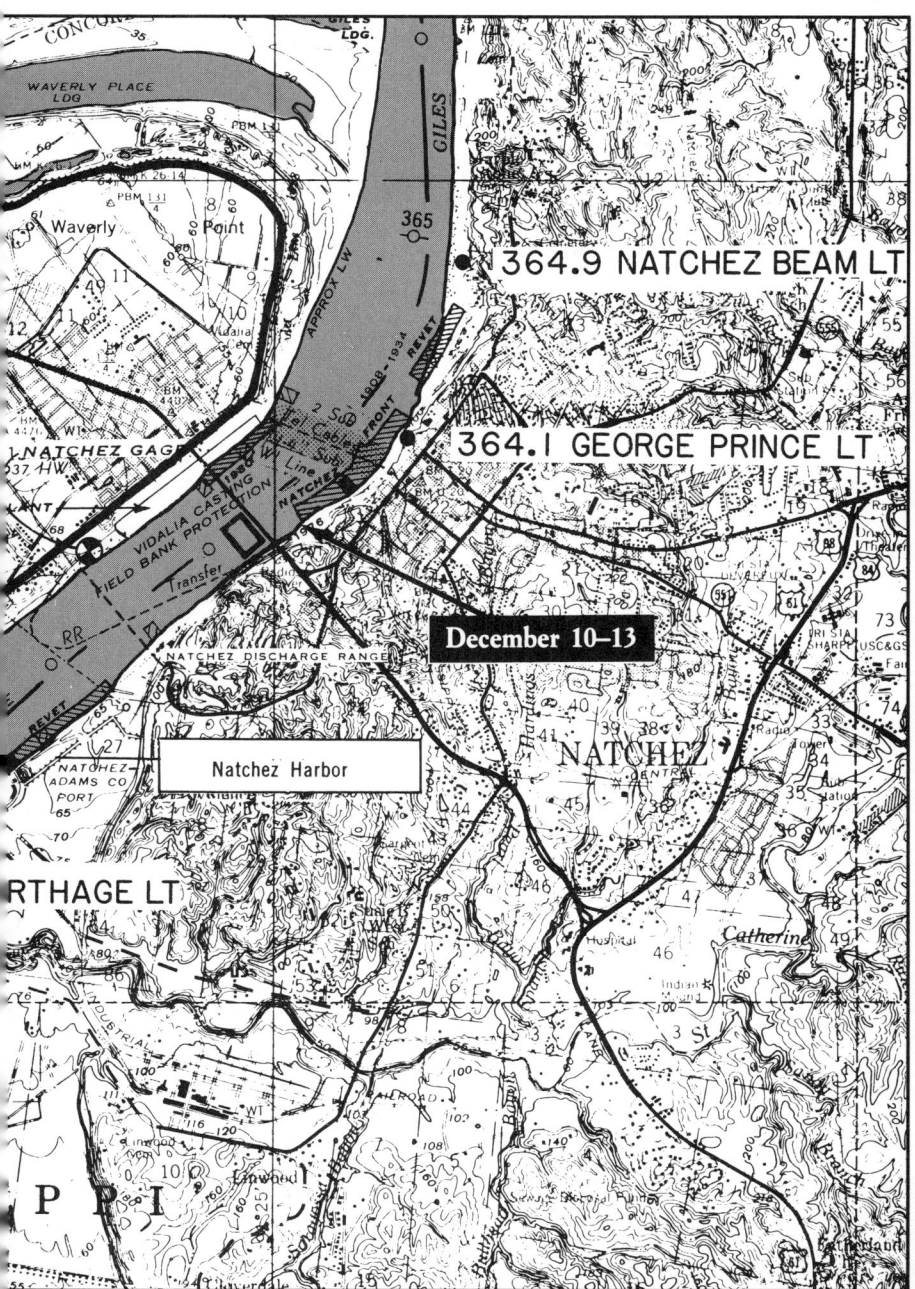

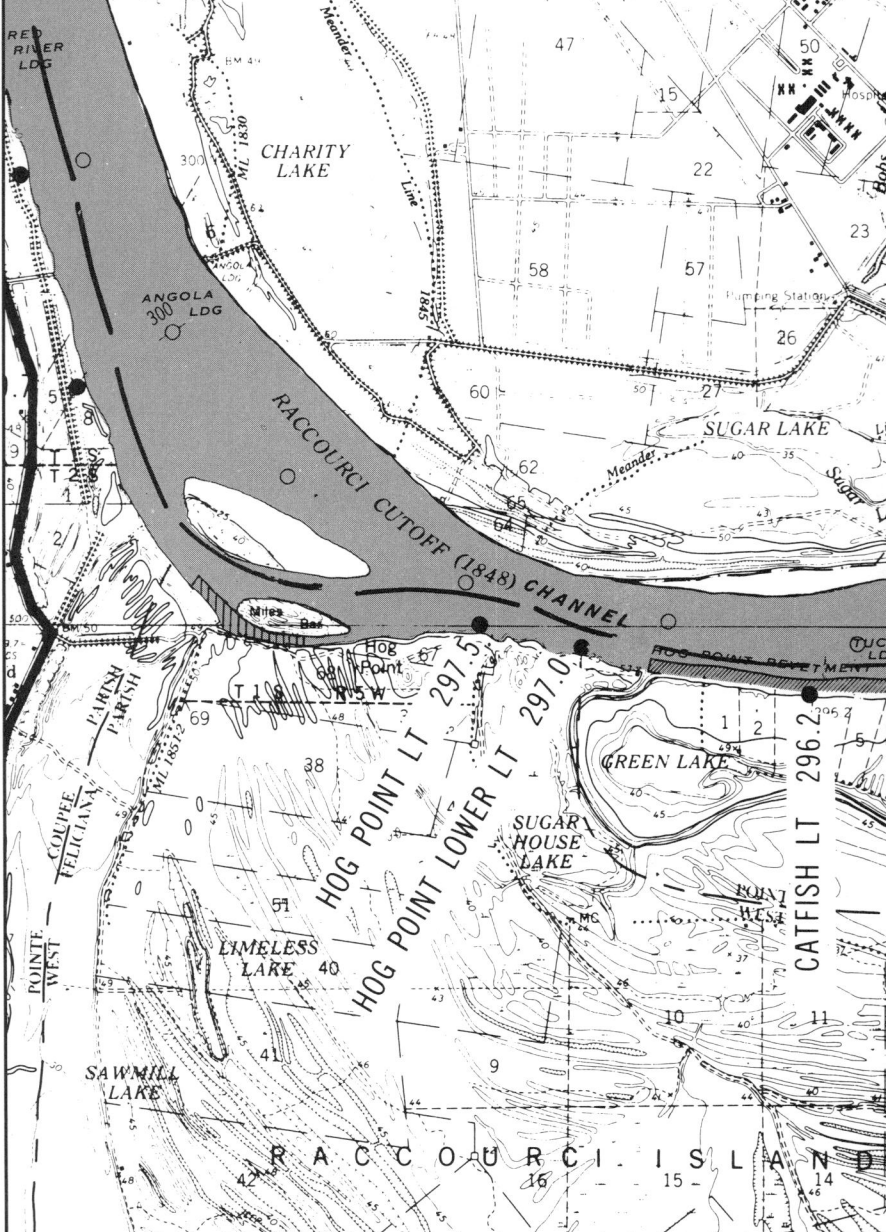

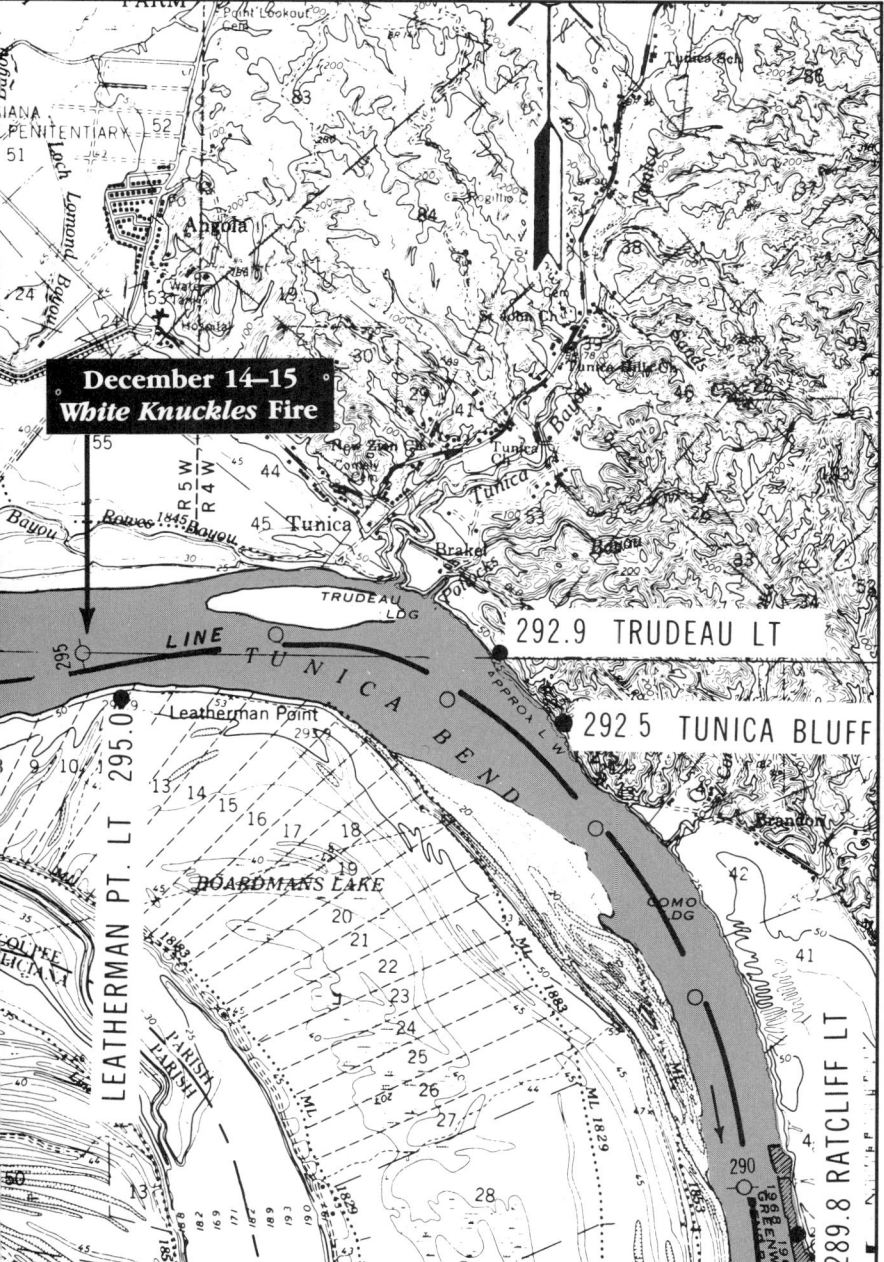

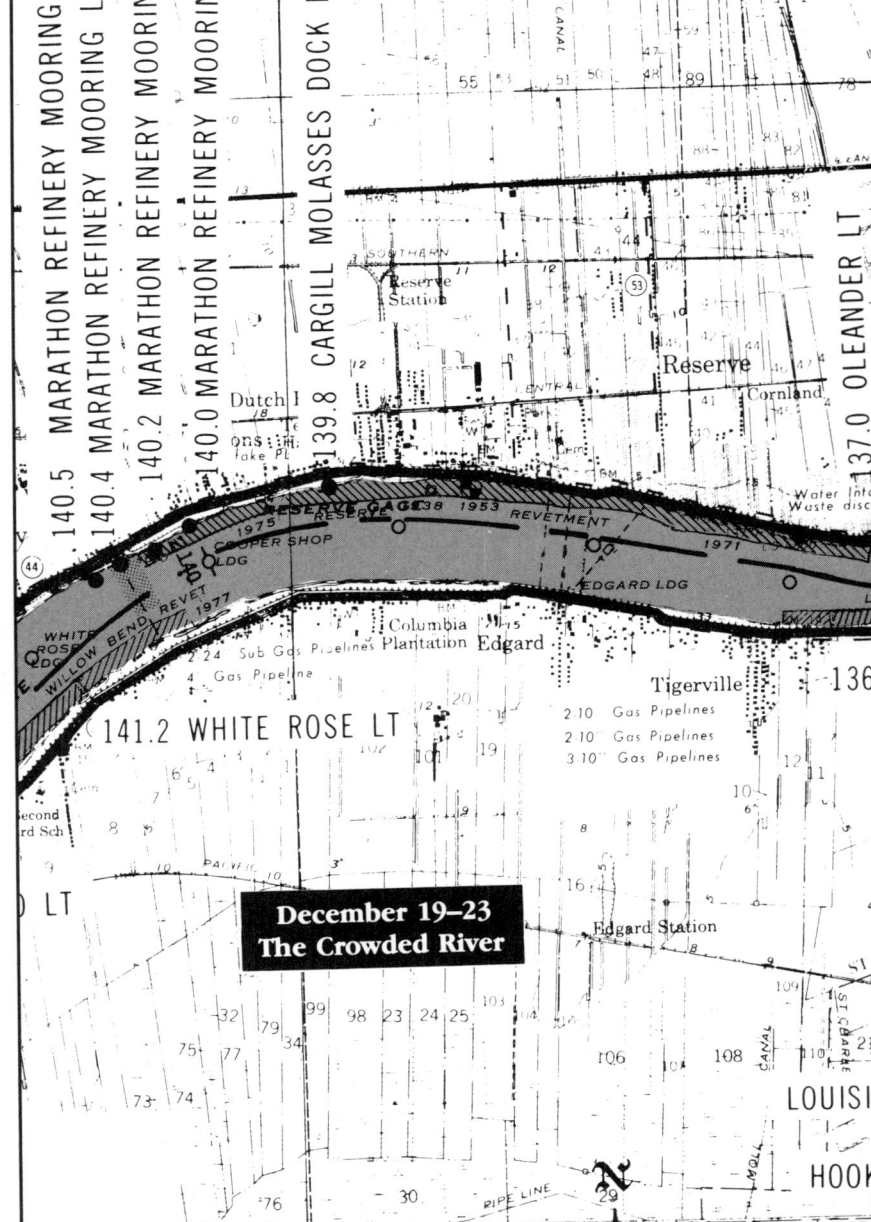

**December 19–23
The Crowded River**

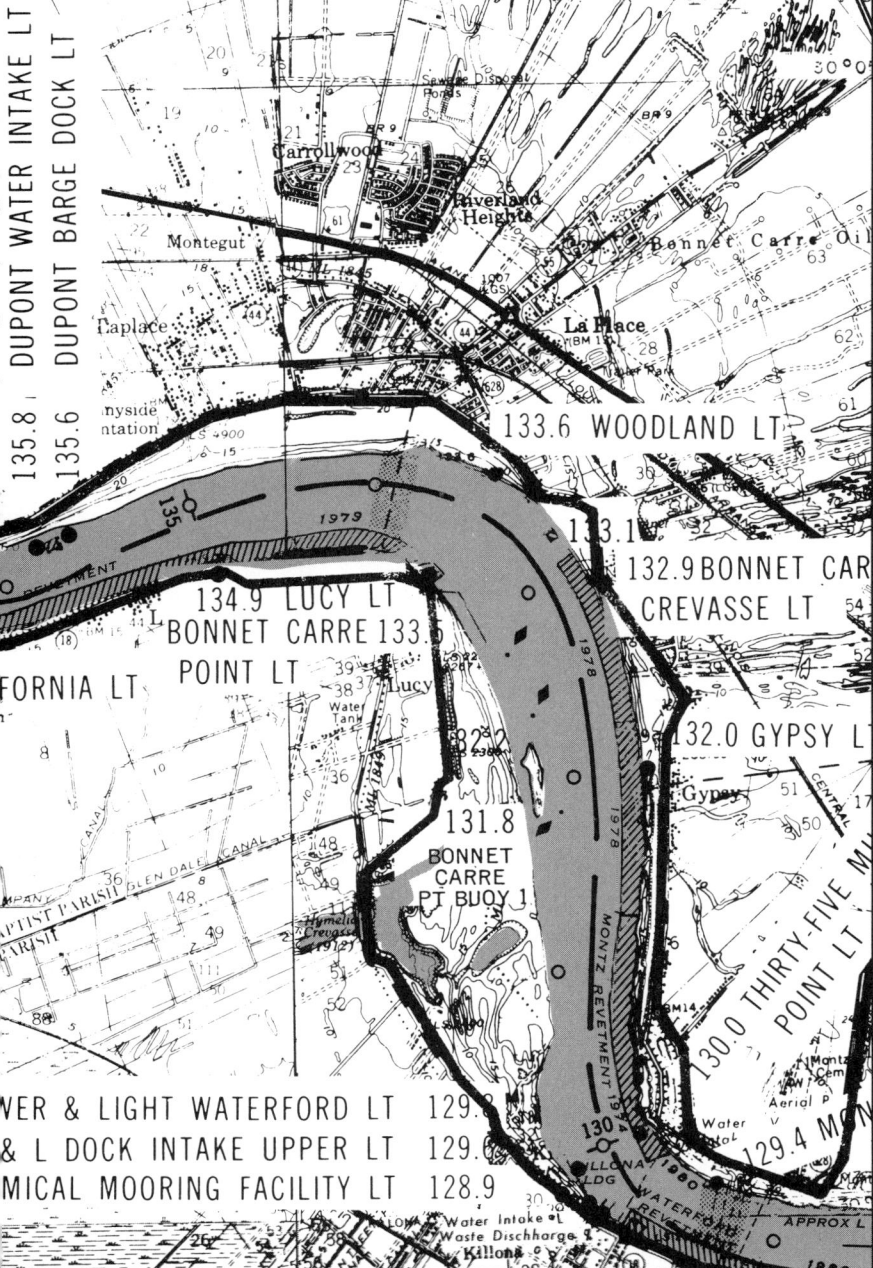

December 14
Mile 295, Mississippi River

Freedom — the freedom of the open river once more! *White Knuckles* and *Gamine* carried us to a quiet anchorage sixty-seven miles below Natchez today, and when the weather finally broke, the sailing proved wonderful indeed. Did I write that I feared I could never sail *White Knuckles* at motor speed? In the brisk winds provided us today, with full main and lapper, *White Knuckles* easily kept up with *Gamine* and her sixteen-horsepower diesel. At one point, *Gamine* passed us, but then the wind improved even more and we passed *Gamine*. By 1500 the wind had increased so much that I dropped the lapper and kept pace with *Gamine* easily, until at last we dropped anchor.

Dick and Junior came over for a supper of cold cuts and took the opportunity to kid me a bit.

"You sure you're not holding out on us about using your motor?" Junior inquired.

"Pure seamanship," I told him. "Watch me instead of your dad for awhile. You'll learn a few things."

We all laughed, and I realized that it was more refreshing than I thought it would be to have some company at last. The talk turned to families, and I learned that Dick is divorced. His wife had gotten pretty tired of being a sailing widow — especially when Junior took to accompanying his father on the longer hauls. Dick made enough money in real estate to retire at fifty, and he was quick to admit that his ex's complaint was legitimate — he'd been on the water virtually all the time since.

"This is my first trip," I confided. "But my wife is pretty understanding."

"And she will be," Dick agreed. "For awhile."

Dick's commentary made me feel guilty. Though I have written to my wife every day, I've called her only infrequently. There's no way to get around the fact that what I'm doing is selfish. We both know it, and thus our telephone conversations tend to be stilted. I've deliberately avoided them, I realize, for this reason.

"I guess it's easy to become married to your boat before you know it," I told Dick.

"Why do you think we give them women's names?" he asked me.

December 15
Baton Rouge, Louisiana

I write tonight from Baton Rouge and, for the second time on this journey, I'm lucky to be here.

I should have known that something was coming from the moment I awoke this morning. It was still quite dark and very cold, and I was surprised to find, upon consulting the clock, that it was only 0430.

Try as I might, I couldn't get back to sleep. I was filled with a sense of impending disaster.

I got up, fixed some breakfast, and killed time for awhile. Dick and Junior and I had agreed upon a 0730 departure, and I knew that they wouldn't be up and around for at least another hour. Finally, unable to shake the sense of dark portent that was weighing upon me, I went up on deck to fill my gas cans. It was just about 0700.

I was filling the second one when, utterly without warning, it exploded in my hands. I hurled it overboard quickly, but as I did, some of the gas spilled into the cockpit locker and ran down into the bilge. In seconds, a fire was blazing away.

Then I looked down in horror to find that my clothing was on fire as well.

I patted at myself furiously with whatever I could find until the flames on me were extinguished, and then I snatched up the fire extinguisher from the cabin. The fire in the cockpit was easy to put out, but it required the entire cylinder in the extinguisher. Now I could see that the cabin was on fire as well, in the bilge. *White Knuckles* was burning!

With no other extinguisher, I resorted to towels. I beat at the flames until I could beat no more, shouting the entire time, talking to my boat. I think I was trying to convey reassurance, even though, at this point, I was sure that all was lost. In the midst of this fracas, a fireman from the marina arrived and began flinging things around, trying to get at the fire. Though we got in each other's way a lot, we finally managed, between the two of us, to get the blaze put out. I sank to the deck, exhausted and scared silly.

"No serious damage," the fireman told me after he had inspected the cabin. "You were lucky. If you hadn't had that fire extinguisher, the whole boat would have gone up."

I looked up at him. He was about my age and build, but he wore a pair of thick glasses which created the effect of magnifying his pupils. Though he probably wasn't thinking any such thing, it seemed that he regarded me with something close to utter reproach.

"It must have been my fault," I told him automatically. "That gas can just exploded. I don't know what I did."

"These things happen," he said. The tone of his voice, I thought, held reproach as well. He pointed. "That ski suit you're wearing," he observed.

"What about it?" I asked. I had put it on this morning against the cold; it was the warmest clothing I had brought with me.

"It's just possible the static electricity that thing generates set off the gasoline," he told me. "I'd watch it, in future."

So that was it, I thought. No wonder my clothing caught fire as well. I nearly killed myself and damaged *White Knuckles* again — this time because I'd worn the wrong clothes. For the third time on this journey, I felt like giving up and turning back. I even felt like mooring *White Knuckles* and catching a plane at Baton Rouge. If I stayed aboard her any longer, I feared I might destroy her.

The fireman departed. We'd never even bothered to

introduce ourselves. Dick and Junior arrived shortly, attracted by the commotion. They'd not even been aware of the explosion. They'd heard it all right, but attributed it to hunters in the nearby woods.

"You'll have to go on without me," I told Dick. "I've got to have some time alone to put this together."

"Think you're the first fellow to ever have his sailboat catch fire?" Dick asked me, and I appreciated his understanding that I needed to be cheered out of my sense of failure.

"No," I told him. "I know I'm not. But I've got to have some time to deal with this. If you want, I'll meet you two at Baton Rouge. Let's just say I'm going to let the boat air out for awhile."

My friends reluctantly agreed, and with assurances from me that I would be only an hour or two behind them, they weighed anchor. As it turned out, it was only thirty minutes before I hoisted *White Knuckles's* sail — this place had meant bad luck for us, and I wanted it far behind me.

White Knuckles and I arrived in Baton Rouge at 1630, both considerably the worse for wear. *Gamine* was already anchored at the marina, and we were able to find a berth not too far away. Light winds had cut our speed for all but the last hour of this haul, but they picked up after that, allowing us to come really booming into port. I spent the day afraid to light a cigarette — and darned sure afraid to wear that ski suit any more. Since the weather has remained chilly, I nearly froze. The old fellow in port at Natchez had been right — it's different down here, and fifty degrees feels cold.

By now I've gotten around to clearing my head and counting our blessings. *White Knuckles* is in one piece, and I am alive. I've been lucky — and I made a resolution to give that luck a cushion by stocking an extra fire extinguisher from this point on. We'll lay over here a couple of days to recoup our losses . . . and to soothe my jangled nerves. I had planned to call my wife tonight; today's news, I feel, she will sleep much better without.

December 16 through 18

The time we have spent in Baton Rouge, rather than turning out to be the recuperative period I had hoped for, has been frustrating and even depressing. Our first mistake was mooring at Red's Boat Store, which is listed in *Quimby's Harbor Guide* as a good stop for small boats. It isn't. There's no gas here, no kerosene — in fact, there's virtually nothing for small boats at all. Red's caters to the tugboat trade, and therefore sells groceries in gallon sizes or more. We don't have much use for a gallon of catsup or pork and beans or soup. Red's is an unfriendly place, too; although someone from here makes numerous trips into town each day, nobody has been interested in picking up anything for me. For six dollars per day, all Red's has supplied is a place to moor — and even that is up against a rusty old barge.

Do I sound cranky? I may be getting that way. Baton Rouge, perhaps because it came so quickly after the fire, hasn't had the best effect on me. On top of that, the weather has stayed bad. And worse, Dick and Junior decided to head for New Orleans yesterday. I hope, of course, to see them there — but I didn't realize I would miss them quite so much.

"Gonna be all right?" Dick asked me as we stood for a few moments on the marina yesterday morning.

"Sure I am," I told him. "I didn't start this trip without any expectations of trouble."

"If that fire turns out to be the worst of your troubles," Dick replied, "you'll go home one lucky fellow."

And that's when I knew that, with the positive experiences I've had so far, I'm going to go home one lucky fellow anyway. Wherever you are, Dick, thanks for the words of encouragement when I needed them.

The first day we spent here was a Sunday, and I do believe that the church bells were the loudest noise I heard all day. Quite a change from Natchez! It was also a lonesome noise to my ears. The Shermans were busy working on their own boat, and I found myself strolling about town, seeing what there was to see. On the grounds of the state capitol, I found a sign which informed me that Baton Rouge was so named by an Indian who spoke French — certainly not uncommon in the history of this area — and that dates from 1699. I also found out that Baton Rouge means *red pole.*

The city has a history of changing hands. Great Britain had it from 1763 to 1779, even though it was first settled by

French trappers. Then Spain took over from 1779 to 1810. At that point, it became part of the Republic of West Florida. It was occupied by Confederate troops during the Civil War. Those very Confederate troops, by the way, set up some buildings to serve as their headquarters, which they called "The Pentagon." Those buildings are still standing.

As for the port itself, it's the busiest one we have yet visited. There are barges everywhere you look — hundreds of barges and almost as many tugboats, which are shuttling barges around to make up tows. It all reminds me of a large railroad switchyard — and, by the way, there are some fifteen or twenty oceangoing ships here as well. This port is as far upriver as they are allowed to travel — but they certainly do come here. I can expect to meet quite a few of them on my way to New Orleans. That's all right. The ones I've seen so far don't create wakes anything like those of the huge tugs.

Last evening, a tugboat captain I met at Red's invited me over to his boat for dinner. We struck up a relationship strong enough to cause him to invite me back for breakfast this morning. During breakfast, I began asking him about his wages. His salary is $180 per day! Even his deckhands earn from $50 to $90 a day.

"Look," I finally said to him, "would you consider giving me a job?" I laughed, but I believe that at this point in my Baton Rouge depression, I was half-serious.

But the captain just lit his pipe and chuckled a bit. "Come to see me when you get hungry," he told me, "or when you get tired of sailing, whichever comes first."

"I'll remember that," I assured him, and then I asked him to forecast some good weather for us.

"Won't happen today," he told me. "Look for things to get rough."

They did. By midmorning a bitter-cold north wind had swept down upon us, dropping the temperature to below freezing in just moments. How long can a cold front last this far south? That remains to be seen.

I bundled up as best I could in the late afternoon and walked toward town. The wind was so cold that I caught the first bus that came along, and a feeling of loneliness in my gut was as forbidding as the weather. I rode that bus to the end of the line and transferred to another one.

"Does this bus run close to a shopping mall?" I asked the driver.

"Yup," he told me. "Will just any shopping mall do?"

"Just any one," I replied, and settled down for the ride. By dusk, I was back on board *White Knuckles* with a shopping bag full of necessary purchases. So much for Red's.

And my mood has got to improve!

December 19 through 23
Mile 113, Mississippi River

The crowded river.

That's what *White Knuckles* and I have experienced for five days now, trying to make our way to New Orleans. I had hoped to make half the distance on the first day. The weather had broken, but even so, no matter which way the now-winding river turned, the wind seemed to head us. If I'd known what was coming, though, I'd have considered the wind a minor problem. We were just around the corner, as it turned out, from heavy traffic.

I saw the first signs of this traffic in the Baton Rouge harbor — and sure enough, on the first day of this hitch I saw no less than four oceangoing ships. They weren't really big ones; I judged them to be about the size of our old Liberty ships from World War II. What surprised me was that not one of them was an American vessel. One was German, one Russian, one Indian, and one Liberian — but not an American ship among them. I took a picture of the German ship; it seemed more patriotic, somehow, than snapping the Russian one.

We anchored that first night next to — of all things — a United States Health Services leper colony. I have to admit I was unaware that there were still lepers in this country. There must be more than a few, to judge from the ferry boat which ran from the colony to the opposite shore every twenty minutes or so.

I had hoped these big ships would not cause the wake

problems that *White Knuckles* and I had been experiencing with the barge tows, and they have not. But as I found out on the second day of this last stint before New Orleans, there is another more formidable difficulty. The river winds badly, and the traffic is ungodly. At one point on that second day, I was dodging no less than five large tows and three big ships at one time. The banks of this river area are utterly lined with oil refineries, chemical plants, and factories. I feel as if *White Knuckles* and I have been plunged into some futuristic movie whose subject is overpopulation.

I've had to use the motor several times. The traffic here also cuts the wind and the currents, and I'm afraid that *White Knuckles* doesn't get the respect that's due her down here. She's just too small. By day three, there was another problem as well — fog. The weather had been so good — sixty-five degrees and up — that I'd just concentrated on the traffic. But three mornings ago I awoke to such heavy fog that there was no visibility at all until about ten in the morning. It gave me a very uneasy feeling; ships of all kinds were packed thick around us, and I couldn't see them. Those ships have their radar, and I kept telling myself that they couldn't possibly run aground. But the news on the radio that very evening told of a ship aground near Donaldsonville — just upriver — due to engine trouble.

The fog continued for three days and ended in a driving rain. It seems to have taken forever to come these last ninety-plus miles. For a sailboat, I have learned, the old right-of-way rule just doesn't apply down here. Ships and barges respect it for each other and for something bigger than they are. But when you're the size of *White Knuckles,* you get little respect and no right-of-way.

I've gotten my nerve back, though. The steering I've done through this heavy traffic has let me know how to take care of my ship. That time we spent in the fog, with the shore 200 feet away but not visible at all, called for all the stamina I had — and I had it. The traffic didn't lick me, and the river didn't, either. The depression I've felt since the fire has all but vanished, and *White Knuckles* and I are ready to sail proudly into New Orleans . . . tomorrow!

Wise old sage of the river that I now am, I'll offer a bit of advice. Here are the priorities to keep in mind while sailing this river, as far as I'm concerned:

1. Barge tows, first and foremost. Their wake alone will ruin you.

2. The current. It shows little predictability, but you've still got to try to outguess it.

3. The charts. Know where you are, all the time. You dare not guess at it.

4. The ships. They're only half as dangerous as the tows, but they're too big to disregard.

5. The weather. It can be your best friend — or your worst enemy.

6. Good strong gear and rigging. You might be able to sail with inferior equipment, but you'll regret it.

7. A first mate — if you can get one.

8. *Two strong options* — for any move you are about to make!

New Orleans — tomorrow, you're ours!

December 24
New Orleans, Louisiana

O r so I thought.

We did make it, but hardly in the manner of a grand entrance. Even so, I could have happily done without that. It was the nearly getting myself killed that bothered me.

It's a funny thing about this river — once you think you've learned all your lessons out here, it's ready to teach you another one, and it usually does. As a case in point, consider our experience of last night. I'd tied up in shallow water near the shore, anticipating New Orleans today and very much wanting a good night's sleep.

As it turned out, I slept a little too well.

Last night was a stormy one, with quite a few strong winds — deceptive because they were of such short duration. It didn't look that bad to me, so I'd tied up without putting out my "insurance anchor."

That, you will remember, is a mistake I swore I'd never make again.

I went to sleep and awoke about 0100 to crashing thunder and a sky alive with lightning. I went on deck to check things out, but all seemed in order and I bedded down again.

At about 0300, I was awakened again — this time not by thunder, but by voices talking loudly. Those voices were alarming enough, but even more alarming was the violent thumping that could be felt against *White Knuckles's* hull.

I stuck my head out in the cockpit and found myself

looking straight at a tugboat, which was tying onto *White Knuckles*. My first thought was, "These guys must be pirates."

But then I made out a figure that certainly didn't appear to be Captain Hook hopping onto our deck. "Hello?" I asked tentatively — and a bit stupidly.

"My name's Swain," the stranger told me, advancing. "And that's my tug. You just wake up?"

"I'm afraid so," I told him, heading for the deck. "What's going on here?"

Once on the deck, I could see that the skies had cleared, leaving all bathed in moonlight. I could also see that my visitor was about sixty, tall and weathered looking.

"Unless I'm very mistaken," he told me now, "you're a good ways down the river from where you thought you were. We found you floating."

"My God," I said. I felt as if he'd struck me.

"It'll happen down here," he said. "Come on over to my tug and have some coffee."

I asked him to give me a minute, and I went back below while Swain boarded his own boat. I sat down on the bunk and put my head in my hands. I must have drifted well over an hour, I thought. *White Knuckles* and I had passed no telling how many barges, boats, and ships — met and somehow passed them all. It was a miracle that we were not run down and smashed. A pure miracle!

The image that occurred to me came from a silent movie in which the comic hero had gone to sleep at the wheel of a car. As the audience watched, the car — sleeping driver snoring away — somehow negotiated an entire downtown area, barely missing other vehicles of every description, running up on the sidewalk and off again, confounding workers in a garage whose doors were open at each end of the building. The comedian, in fact, never woke up until his car ran off a dock and into the river.

Into the river.

I'd been that comic hero, I realized — not a real sailor, but some clown trying to navigate water restricted to professionals. Just like that silent-movie clown, I'd slept blissfully while all manner of peril narrowly avoided me, protected by a divine hand.

The Lord looks out for children and fools.

I felt rotten, far worse than after the fire. I trudged over to thank Swain and his crew as if I were condemned.

Swain's crew consisted of his wife and son. They were nice people who nevertheless couldn't cover for the fact that I hadn't anchored myself properly. I drank coffee with them, thanked them, and very thankfully returned to my own boat. The sense of confidence reborn I'd had just last night had vanished. I was going to be unfit company for awhile.

A nice attitude to bring to New Orleans, huh? It certainly didn't help things. We made the Piety Street Wharf at about 1400, and my mood had blackened. It figures, then, that I'd wind up docking in exactly the wrong place.

In that wharf, I realized after only a few moments, things were going to be much too crowded. Ships, barges, and pilot boats were pounding *White Knuckles* against the pilings of the wharf steadily, and before long, two mooring lines were snapped. Next we sustained dented fenders and a badly bent cleat, and I was ready to leave. That kind of treatment can ruin a small boat in a very short time.

We tried the Canal Street Wharf next, which proved to be even worse. *White Knuckles* hardly needed worse treatment. I was feeling the worse for wear, too. Though the Swain family had taken us over to some empty barges tied to a bank and left us to rest, I couldn't sleep. I couldn't even sit still. By that point I'd learned that I had drifted six miles last night. I had simply sat and shuddered until 0900. And now I was feeling tiredness creep over me.

I thought briefly about going ashore — forgetting my troubles in the bright lights of New Orleans — but I quickly saw that it would be impossible in these wharves. Once you tie up to one of the wharves — if you can — the things are so tall that there is no way to get up onto the apron of the wharf. There are no ladders. Nobody makes any provisions for small boats down here — or for those who sail them.

White Knuckles and I finally came across the river, behind a long row of ships awaiting pilots, and anchored. I have decided to go back across the river and take an industrial lock. I must get into either Lake Pontchartrain or Lake Borgne quickly. I'm down to one day's water supply and about two days' food. I've got one gallon of gas left, and I'm feeling cranky as hell.

It's time to check this day in and hope that things go better tomorrow. I plan to get off the river and take the inland waterway east from New Orleans. Many, many lives have been claimed by this river — and mine was almost one of them very early this morning.

As I sacked in, I realized it was Christmas Eve. Had I been able to go ashore, I most certainly would have called my wife. She probably spent the evening doing those things which make for a good Christmas Eve — being with friends and family, exchanging gifts, reminiscing over holidays past . . . .

Maybe I wouldn't have called her, after all. When I think about it, the last thing she needs tonight is me.

December 25

White Knuckles and I spent this day, Christmas, 1979, at anchor. I didn't have a present for *White Knuckles,* and she didn't have one for me. I haven't even had time to say "Bah" or "Humbug," if truth be told. I've spent the day trying to get the attention of someone — *anyone* on the shore. We are, in effect, stranded.

But no small boats showed all day, and no one came by the shore. Every sane person up there must be home with loved ones — or celebrating Christmas New Orleans-style. I know quite well that I probably couldn't get gas or charts today anyway, but . . . .

But I long for some human companionship.

It's not that the anchorage itself is bad. We're behind a long row of ships anchored closely together in line. This line has the effect of protecting us from the traffic in the main channel. *White Knuckles* is tied to a small bush sticking about halfway out of the water, and I also have a stern anchor and bow anchor out. There's going to be no more drifting.

River people do, of course, look after their own kind, and in the late afternoon a pilot boat did come alongside. The skipper was a youngish fellow with a bristly black beard. He asked me what the trouble was, and I told him I needed gas and charts and was running low on food. He went below his deck to scare up somebody on the radio, stayed awhile, and returned looking downcast.

"What's the word?" I asked him.

"Coast Guard won't help," he replied glumly. "They say there's no apparent distress involved."

"Great," I said. "Thanks anyway. And Merry Christmas."

We parted ways, and I went below feeling even lonelier. I can dink ashore in the morning and get my supplies, so I guess it really is more loneliness than anything else. I'm shot and need some rest. I've turned in a rather bad performance during the past forty-eight hours. That's enough to get anybody down on a Christmas Day.

Later, as the stars came out, I went back on deck and looked at the line of ships which spreads out from *White Knuckles* and me. There are about thirty — although that's pure guess, because they stretch around a bend in the river. Most of them are foreign, and, as I remember from earlier today, Panama is the country most frequently represented. But I know a lot of our ships register with Panama to avoid the stricter U.S. rules and taxes. Almost all these ships are tankers, and they're empty. Are we exporting oil, or what?

After a time I gave up such speculation and instead considered all those ships as guests of *White Knuckles* and me for a Christmas party on the river. It didn't work. I still felt lonely — and for the first time, really anxious to be off this river.

But I raised my coffee cup to that line of ships in mock toast anyway, smiling a rueful smile.

"Merry Christmas, my international friends," I told the empty ships and the stars and the night. "Bah. Humbug."

DECEMBER 26
Lake Pontchartrain

We are safe tonight, moored at the Southern Yacht Club on Lake Pontchartrain. No — we haven't suddenly escalated in class; *White Knuckles* and I just made another mistake, but this time a happy one.

Let me start with this morning. I awoke to a clear, bright day, feeling somewhat less grumpy than I had the night before. While I was having my coffee, a pilot boat came alongside, captained by a ruddy-faced young man named Jack Chase, who looked as though he had quite literally spent his life on the river. We visited, and he offered to take me ashore for my gasoline and supplies. That, of course, is when the day really brightened up.

Though Jack must have been at least twenty years younger than I am, I couldn't help but find a sort of example in him. As we headed for shore, I studied his hands and face, both scarred by wind and weather. He'd paid his dues to the water, but he was comfortable here now, far more comfortable than I was. I asked him if he lived on the river.

"Don," he told me, "I wouldn't even be able to sleep on dry land."

I understood that I was in the process of paying my dues now and that it was a process that could go on for some time yet — if I stuck it out. I looked around at the brilliant, sunlit water and at the hundreds of boats in harbor. Then I looked back toward the boats that were outward bound.

I knew again, with utter clarity, how badly I wanted to stick it out.

Getting the supplies took most of the morning, and I got my first real look at New Orleans, by bus, as it turned out. But I was anxious to get *White Knuckles* out of her rather precarious location, so I hurried back with Jack Chase, who had agreed to meet me for the return trip. By noon, *White Knuckles* and I had entered the industrial canal that leads to Lake Pontchartrain and were on our way.

We went through one lock and under three drawbridges, traveling a total of eight miles in the course of the afternoon. We entered the lake about an hour before sundown, at which point I set our sights on a marina just to the left of the lake entrance.

That's how our happy mistake came about.

It grew dark, and I overshot, mistaking this yacht club for the marina. It's a darned ritzy place, and they could well have turned me away — but whether from Christmas-spirit hangover or maybe just plain pity, they didn't. *White*

Knuckles and I are sleeping in style tonight.

The day after Christmas 1979 has proved a good one for me — a time of renewal. I have more scars to get, I know, to keep up this life on the river, but tonight I find myself willing to do so. I reflect on our adventures thus far, and I know that whatever else might come during the short remainder of 1979, I have done what I've always wanted to do. I have followed my dream and sailed in *White Knuckles,* worthy and true, down the Mississippi River to New Orleans.

By the gods of the seven seas, we made it!

December 27, 1979, to January 9, 1980

I abandoned my daily log entries a little less than two weeks ago — since we found a slip at the Municipal Yacht Harbor — and so I have some catching up to do. It is 2000 on a downright balmy evening, and I'm spending my last bit of time on *White Knuckles* for awhile.

My wife arrives at midnight tonight.

I've made reservations at a motel for us, and I've rented a car. We're going to do New Orleans up big, and I want things to be right. She'd never be comfortable on *White Knuckles.*

Am I excited — anxious to see her? You're darned right I am. I've been far too long without her.

Why, then, do I feel so wistful at this moment? Why have I taken this time to make what will be my final entry for this leg of my journey? Why am I looking around at these all-too-familiar cabin walls with such a bittersweet sadness?

I've got precious little time to shake this mood — and thus I've decided to write myself out of it.

New Orleans has been an experience indeed. The day after our royal stay at the yacht club, the harbormaster of the Municipal Yacht Harbor advised me that he could rent me a slip for *White Knuckles* only on a day-to-day basis — the harbor was just too crowded. What this came down to was an indefinite stay here — as long as we were willing to move from slip to slip as other owners took their boats out. That sounded fine to me; I'd already fallen in love with this place, and downtown New Orleans was only thirty minutes away.

Downtown New Orleans! I've explored it now from the far end of Bourbon Street through the French Quarter to the end of the streetcar line. At first I walked, but after a week of that I bought a bicycle. It's a bit of a foreign experience for me to ride it — I haven't been on one in years. I find it a contrary device, particularly in the wind. It doesn't tack worth a darn.

It is, of course, bowl-game time here — and the streets downtown are filled with football fans from Arkansas and Alabama. The city is accommodating them with everything from appropriate T-shirts and hats to red beer in the bars. I'm not much of a football fan, I'm afraid, so my sports activities have been limited to one trip to the horse races — a bit of foolishness I enjoyed but could easily have done without.

Far more enjoyable was the bus ride I took last Saturday down to the French Quarter, where I strolled around looking at a lot of history in the form of old buildings. There are no cars allowed on the streets down there during the day, and so that's where I walked — along with every Sugar Bowl tourist in town, that is.

Believe it or not, I was one of the few in the throng without a camera! Assuming me to be a local, people asked me for directions time after time. Maybe I'm at last starting to look like the sort of grizzled sailor who calls this place home — when he's in port!

I went to one of the yacht clubs for a drink, too, at the invitation of the skipper of the boat moored next to *White Knuckles*. That was a dreary experience, despite the fact that it was New Year's Eve. It seemed that everybody in the bar was already drunk, even though it was midafternoon. The noise, the smoke, and the music depressed me, and I longed for *White Knuckles's* cabin.

Perhaps I have been alone too much. That certainly is a situation that will be corrected in just a few hours.

Even so, I am surprised, looking back on my days here, by how much time I've spent in the harbor. Lake Pontchartrain itself is a fascinating body of water. It's very large, of course, but also shallow — no more than ten to fourteen feet in depth. On a windy day — and I've seen a few in the time I've been here — this lake can be rough. Boats have been lost here, and many people have drowned over the years. Why? Because they have underestimated the forces of nature at work in the water. I'm told, incidentally, that things are not nearly so crowded on the other side of the lake and that the rates are not so high. I may wind up going north across the lake before I leave here to take a look at Slidell and Madisonville.

Did I say crowded? What an understatement! The Orange Bowl Regatta is under way in this very harbor, and there are boats here from all over the United States. I've never seen so many sailboats in one place before — thousands of them, as far as the eye can see. The Municipal Yacht Club itself is so large that it is divided into an east end and a west end, and there doesn't seem to be an inch in either direction that isn't occupied by a sailboat. Some represent colleges; some are just individually owned. But they are everywhere.

The camaraderie of sailboat owners is something rare and wonderful. I've spent four or five days — all of which flew by — visiting along the rows of boats, making new friends and swapping sailing adventures. *White Knuckles* and I are at home here and hardly anxious to leave. To a great extent, I don't even want to leave this slip. Perhaps that is the reason for the near homesickness — homesickness over leaving this cabin — which fills me tonight.

I met a man a few days ago who came all the way from Minnesota in a canoe. In truth, he came in two canoes. He had rigged an arrangement in which the two were bolted together about eight feet apart with a plywood platform between them. It was on this platform that he erected his tent at night. The man's name was Clyde Gragg, and I came to consider him, after listening to his stories, as a latter-day Leatherstocking.

Clyde told me he had traveled to St. Louis on the first

leg of his journey by paddling and drifting. Then he had purchased a small outboard motor that he mounted between the canoes. From Vicksburg onward, he hitched a lift on a houseboat and cut his time down considerably. He made the journey in two months, and he's ready to go again.

Perhaps Clyde's journey doesn't sound overly rigorous, but for him, it had to be. He's a Vietnam veteran who lost a leg from the knee down in that ugly, fruitless conflict. He supports his travels with disability payments — like me, he's following a dream. His spirit and sheer guts inspire me. I asked him, over a drink that first night, about his future plans.

"To sleep on the water," he told me. "Me and Dutch." Dutch is a playful collie puppy who was just weaned when Clyde left Minnesota. This is the only life the dog has ever known.

"I have to ask," I told Clyde. "How do you housebreak a dog on a boat?"

Clyde threw back his head and laughed. Like many another Vietnam vet, he now sports a full beard and shoulder-length hair. "I wish I knew," he roared. "I wish I knew."

Dutch, of course, just looked sheepish — or as sheepish as a dog can look.

I've spent the past few days trimming ship. A good inspection of *White Knuckles* revealed quite a few scars — one bent cleat, a broken fairlead, and various chips and scratches. All in all, considering the bumbling skipper she's had, she's come through this pretty well. I've been responsible for three ruined bumpers, two lost anchors, and several broken mooring lines. But I think we came through in good condition — *White Knuckles* better than me, although I'm feeling like a pretty fair sailor myself this evening.

This morning I started thinking about how in the world I was going to store that bicycle on board, and I got to wondering if I didn't really need a bigger boat. A twenty-five-footer is as large as I would ever want to handle, especially on my budget. I dismissed the thought quickly — *White Knuckles* and I have got quite a few miles to travel together yet.

There's still quite a bit to do in order to get *White Knuckles* seaworthy for the remainder of the trip — I need to find a boat yard where I can get her hoisted, for one thing. She needs saltwater anti-fouling paint on her bottom, and she needs to get her topside cleaned as well. There's supposedly a place about fifteen miles down the Intracoastal Waterway that can help us out on this. I hope so. Girl deserves some brand-new makeup — and a whole lot more.

I wish I had more carpentering skills. I visited Carl Davis who, with his family from Kansas, is aboard a forty-three-foot catamaran. Carl built their yacht himself, from lofting the lines to rigging it. It took him seven years, working in his spare time. He did an excellent piece of work. I frankly can't tell that boat from a factory-built one. He's working at a boat-repair shop here now, trying to get together enough money for them to cruise to the Bahamas — which is *their* dream. At least, it's their immediate one.

Carl believes they could work here and there at boat repair and ultimately cruise around the world. After looking over the boat he built, I believe they'll make it.

I received the letter two days ago which let me know that my wife would soon meet me here. She included pictures of my new baby granddaughter and season's greetings from everyone back home. Tonight I wait for the time to come when I will pick her up at the airport. I've missed her — and all of them.

I'll miss you for a few days, too, *White Knuckles.* We're at the end of our first successful journey together and, in some ways, I've come to feel more at home in this cabin than I've felt anywhere. But there's water to travel out there yet. You be the same fine boat you've been — and I'll do my best to be a better skipper.

I've got to sign off now and head for the airport. Enjoy your rest, Girl.

January 13
Bayou Sauvage, Louisiana

Tonight *White Knuckles* is moored at B.A.W. Marine on Bayou Sauvage, just off the Intracoastal Waterway between Lake Saint Catherine and Lake Borgne. She's in for some touching up, and then we'll be off on the next leg of our journey.

There is, of course, an old superstition that forbids starting a voyage on the thirteenth — but we had a mere eighteen miles to travel from Lake Pontchartrain, and I decided to disregard it. The short trip was made in a cold mist, but there was only a mild wind and therefore things were bearable. My plan is to put in here for a couple of days while *White Knuckles* gets her face-lift (or bottom-lift, in this case), then sail for Pascagoula, Mississippi, where we will visit my brother who lives in nearby Escatawpa. That will take no more than one or two days, and then we're on the open water again!

I had worried about carrying the bicycle I bought in New Orleans, but it proved to be no problem. I removed the pedals, turned the handlebars lengthwise to the bike, and lashed it upright at the starboard rail to a stanchion and the aft lower shroud. The jib sheet passes between the wheels of the bike, and there is room to go forward between the bike and the cabin top. I've now got sails, a motor, and wheels. I'm mobile.

The time I spent with my wife is something I will hold very close to me for the rest of this journey — for the rest of my life, in fact. We saw New Orleans, we ate and drank — but mostly we simply enjoyed being together. I asked her once again to chuck it all and hop on this boat with me, and she once again told me that she wasn't made for the water. But that did not diminish the time we spent together — not at all.

"Melba," I told her at our airport good-bye, a downright tearful occasion, "I'll owe you this trip for the rest of my life."

She smiled. I am sure now that she understands that I have spent a lifetime in anticipation of this trip. I'm very lucky. Few other people would possess that kind of understanding.

New Orleans grew strangely lonely after she had departed. I waited around a few days longer, buying supplies and trimming ship. I even tried going downtown a few more times. But now the streets I walked and the places I stopped were those we had enjoyed together just a day or two before. Glad as I was to be out of that motel and back on *White Knuckles,* I knew that New Orleans would fill me with sadness now. I made haste to depart.

This area of Louisiana is all marsh, and if it were not for the tall grass it would be difficult to know if you were in the canal or not. The water in the canal stands utterly level with the water and land on each side. Most houses along the canal sit on pilings from four to ten feet tall. We even passed a most exclusive neighborhood named Venetian Isles, where each large brick home has its own canal leading up to a two-boat garage. That's living, huh?

We also encountered our first swing bridges on the way

here — bridges whose center span swivels on a huge turntable to let ships pass. I like them better than the drawbridges we had become so used to — they're just plain easier to navigate.

January 14
Bayou Sauvage, Louisiana

The boat yard workers hoisted *White Knuckles* early this morning with a traveling hoist — the mast did not have to be lowered — and they parked the boat where I could hook up to electricity and water. They furnished me with a ladder so I could come and go inside the boat while they worked on it. The boat's bottom was in better condition than I had expected. One bad gouge was on the keel, where the forked tree rode the anchor train down while we were on the Mississippi. Two coats of bottom paint and a new waterline stripe will cost me $500, which seems outrageous. It makes me wonder if I can actually afford this boat. They would have allowed me to do the work myself, but there would have been a ten-dollars-per-day dock charge, and the paint was thirty-five dollars a quart. Having no paint or cleaning equipment, I elected to let them do the work. I found two small barnacles on the boat's bottom. I suppose they attached themselves there on Lake Pontchartrain; I saw barnacles on the dock pilings there. The water there is about half seawater, half freshwater.

January 15, 1980

The boat yard finished the work on *White Knuckles* at about noon today and set her back into her natural element. I noticed immediately how much easier she glided through the water as we traversed the three miles back to the waterway. We then continued east along the waterway until about 1600, when storm clouds moved in and it began to get ominously dark. Quickly we found an offshoot canal and anchored in about five feet of water. There was not room for the boat to swing at anchor, so I took a bowline ashore and put two stern anchors out. The reason for so many lines is that when a tow of barges passes, the water is drawn out of these side canals, then rushes back in, causing a lot of rolling, pitching, and skittering about. The boat first tries to go out into the waterway, then tries to run back to shore.

The tide in this area is only about one foot, but I am amazed at what a current it sets up in some places. I noticed a strong current at the swing bridges and another one at the junction of two canals. This whole part of Louisiana is laced with waterways, canals, and bayous, all connecting at one place or another. I'm sure one could go anywhere in this part of the state in a shallow-draft boat. I saw a lot of people in boats today, but never saw a house, a barn, or any living thing along the shore. The grass and what I think is cane hide the view. I think it is all swampland in any case, and I doubt if anyone lives along the waterway here.

This canal is only 12 feet deep and 150 feet wide, and we have about twenty more miles of it. Then we'll be in the open water of Mississippi Sound, near Bay Saint Louis and Pass Christian.

January 16
Mississippi Sound

Today at noon, *White Knuckles* found the sea toward which she has been thrusting her bow since November 3, 1979.

I had meant to sail on to Pass Christian, Mississippi, today, but this whole area came under severe local thunderstorms which are supposed to continue through tomorrow. When we reached the Rigolets — an entrance to Pontchartrain from the east — it was raining very hard. We ducked into Little Lake, intending to anchor there and wait out these thunderstorms. I could find no suitable anchorage, so we continued on east across Little Lake, emerged from it past a railroad swing bridge into Mississippi Sound near Heron Bay, and anchored near the L & N Railroad in about thirty feet of water. It was, and still is, raining heavily — which should not stop a sailor — but since this is my first experience with open water, I am reluctant to begin this experience under stormy conditions. The wind is from the south and very warm. I suppose the warm moist wind is causing all this rain. The temperature yesterday was seventy degrees; today it is seventy-five degrees. We brought a boat load of Louisiana mosquitoes into Mississippi, and they are as large and as vicious as I have always been told they are. This is the first time I've been bothered with any insects since this trip began. I did not expect mosquitoes in January, so I have no repellent aboard.

I am oh, so glad to be out of rivers, waterways, and canals. I can now hope to stay on one tack for hours instead of minutes, and I have room to dodge the shipping. I have no idea what open-water sailing will be like, but I'm sure it will be better than what we have been through to get here. My spirits are high, although I must confess to a certain amount of apprehension. "God, thy sea is so great, my boat, so small."

January 17

Hard rain — spiced with short, strong wind gusts — prevailed all day, so we stayed at anchor, waiting for what is supposed to be better weather tomorrow. The temperature today was seventy-five degrees because a cool front moved in from the north, setting off all these thunderstorms. I am thankful it is not cold as well as wet. Tomorrow may be cold and dry. By lying here, I will be running short of water and food to make Pascagoula. I may have to call at Pass Christian, which is only about twenty-five miles from here.

January 18
Near Pass Christian, Mississippi

Today dawned bright and clear, so we weighed anchor early and headed east. As the sun warmed the water, a fog began forming, and finally it brought our visibility so low I knew I could never see the next buoy. I circled the last buoy for some time, but soon tired of that and tied to it, waiting for the fog to lift. (Dear reader, never tie to a buoy — it's against the law.)

In midafternoon the fog lifted enough for me to make out the landmarks of Pass Christian, so we headed in toward port. About three or four miles out, the fog closed in again, so I moved out of the shipping lane and dropped anchor. I hung the anchor light high in the rigging and promptly went to sleep. Just before dozing off, I thought how proud I was of that anchor lantern. It's a good, old American-made storm lantern that I picked up, used, for five dollars. It replaced a solid-brass, British-made one that cost me sixty dollars and would not burn more than thirty minutes without smoking and going out. Small things can mean a great deal at times.

January 19
Biloxi, Mississippi

The fog of last night stayed with us until noon today. Finally I hoisted sail at 1300 and moved out without going ashore at Pass Christian. I was down to one gallon of water but felt it would surely last to Biloxi or possibly Pascagoula. The wind was too light, however, to make Pascagoula, so we came into the Broadwater Marina at Biloxi at about 2000. It was low tide, and the boat touched bottom entering the marina, bumping on in as if knowing how anxious I was to call it a day. It was very good to get moored and tied into electricity and water. I promptly telephoned my wife because I had been unable to mail any letters for a while. She said I had mail waiting at my brother's house in Escatawpa.

January 20

I lazed about today, sitting on the beach watching children at play, the sea birds diving, and the boats coming and going. The Broadwater Marina here is known far and wide as one of the best places in the world to berth a boat. I had read of it in cruising magazines and books, and it does indeed fit all the nice descriptions written about it. Well-kept grounds add to the beauty of the paved docks, each with its own parking space for a car. Laundry, restrooms including showers, courtesy rides to town, and telephones available to each boat are a few of the conveniences offered. I'm sorely tempted to linger at such a place. Tomorrow I should force myself to lay in needed supplies and get ready for departure the next day. However . . . .

January 24
Pascagoula, Mississippi

White Knuckles, bounding under full main and Genoa sails, made good time today from Biloxi to Pascagoula. We are about two miles up the Pascagoula River, moored to an old abandoned dock just below the drawbridge. We reached the bridge at about 1600, but the operator told me he could not let us pass until 1730, so I elected to wait until morning.

When we sailed this morning the weather report called for fifteen- to twenty-knot winds and seas five to seven feet, both diminishing during the day. The wind did not slacken, nor did the seas, at least as far as I could notice. It was a pretty wild sleigh ride into Pascagoula. The waters of this area are shallow, and a wind can build up heavy seas in short order. Yesterday seven- to ten-foot seas were predicted, so I decided to wait one more day. I spent the day shopping and taking in a movie.

The day before that, I did some sight-seeing by bicycle, mostly up and down the road that clings to the beach. The beaches all along here are as white as sugar, very beautiful, and clean. All in all we spent four days in Biloxi, and I still did not want to leave, but I thought of places ahead that may be just as nice, just as beautiful and restful.

Tomorrow we will continue on up the river and get as close to Escatawpa as possible. The chart has ended, so I do not know how much farther we can go. I'm sure we can get as far as Moss Point, which is on the Escatawpa River, as is Escatawpa itself.

January 25
Moss Point, Mississippi

Awakening early this morning, I quickly readied the boat for an attempt to get under the drawbridge before traffic got heavy on it. We approached it at 0640 and gave our three long blasts, but the operator waved us back and yelled out the window that he would open the bridge at 0750. I thanked him and returned to our mooring until the appointed time.

We cleared the bridge promptly at 0750 and continued up the Pascagoula River. It is a well-marked channel, although very winding. Each side is lined with shipbuilding and related industries. A very large paper mill is in operation here, belching great clouds of smoke into the air. A few miles upstream, the Pascagoula is no longer navigable, but the Escatawpa River, which joins the Pascagoula, is. At that junction we turned to starboard and soon reached a swing bridge on Highway 63. After clearing the bridge we took a hard starboard turn and within a few minutes were moored at the Moss Point city dock. Upon inquiry, I discovered we were only one-and-a-half miles from my brother John's home. I quickly assembled the bicycle and peddled to his house, just missing breakfast.

January 26

My older brother John and his wife Daisy showed me around Escatawpa, Moss Point, and Pascagoula today. This area was in the eye of Hurricane Frederic last September 7. Frederic was most devastating, and the evidence is still visible. Many businesses have not yet reopened, due to lost roofs and walls and the slowness of federal financial aid in getting here. Even some state, county, and city buildings are still in need of repair or rebuilding. Shattered homes are still to be seen, some of them beyond repair.

When the hurricane was threatening, some of Daisy's relatives insisted that she and John stay with them during the storm. They did so, and their host's home was heavily damaged, while John and Daisy's house was hardly hurt at all.

All existing marinas here were totally destroyed, so there is no place to moor a boat for services or repair. The mayor of Moss Point told me they had just removed all the sunken boats from the city-dock area and would bend the rules and permit me to stay at their dock for two nights, which was very kind of him. He strongly recommended that I sleep on the boat in case of unwelcome visitors.

>JANUARY 27
>*Pascagoula, Mississippi*

This being my last day at my brother's, I asked him if he would like to come with me for part of this journey. He quickly admitted he would like nothing better, so we began preparing for our departure. About midafternoon *White Knuckles* and I came down to Pascagoula while John finished his last-minute shopping. He is to meet us here early tomorrow. By bringing the boat on and getting past the three bridges, the three of us will be able to clear port quickly come morning. The forecast calls for ten- to fifteen-knot winds from the north with two- to three-foot seas. Sounds like an ideal day in store tomorrow. We will sail for Pensacola, Florida, bypassing Mobile, Alabama.

January 28
Dauphin Island, Alabama

This morning we cleared Pascagoula by 1000, and it looked as though we'd have a good sail reaching by the north wind. However, by 1300 the wind shifted to the east and put us on a beat, slowing our progress considerably. By dark we had barely entered Mobile Bay, so we moved in close to Dauphin Island and anchored in twenty feet of water. This shallow water is rough, and John is uneasy about the tossing we're taking. After all, he's never been on a voyage before.

January 29
Bon Secour, Alabama

Head winds slowed our progress again today. We beat on across Mobile Bay, then out of the waterway to this small town. It is a shrimper village that was almost totally destroyed by Hurricane Frederic in September 1979. We did find some pilings to moor to, which pleased John very much. We are in a small bay, however, and a comfortable anchorage would have been possible.

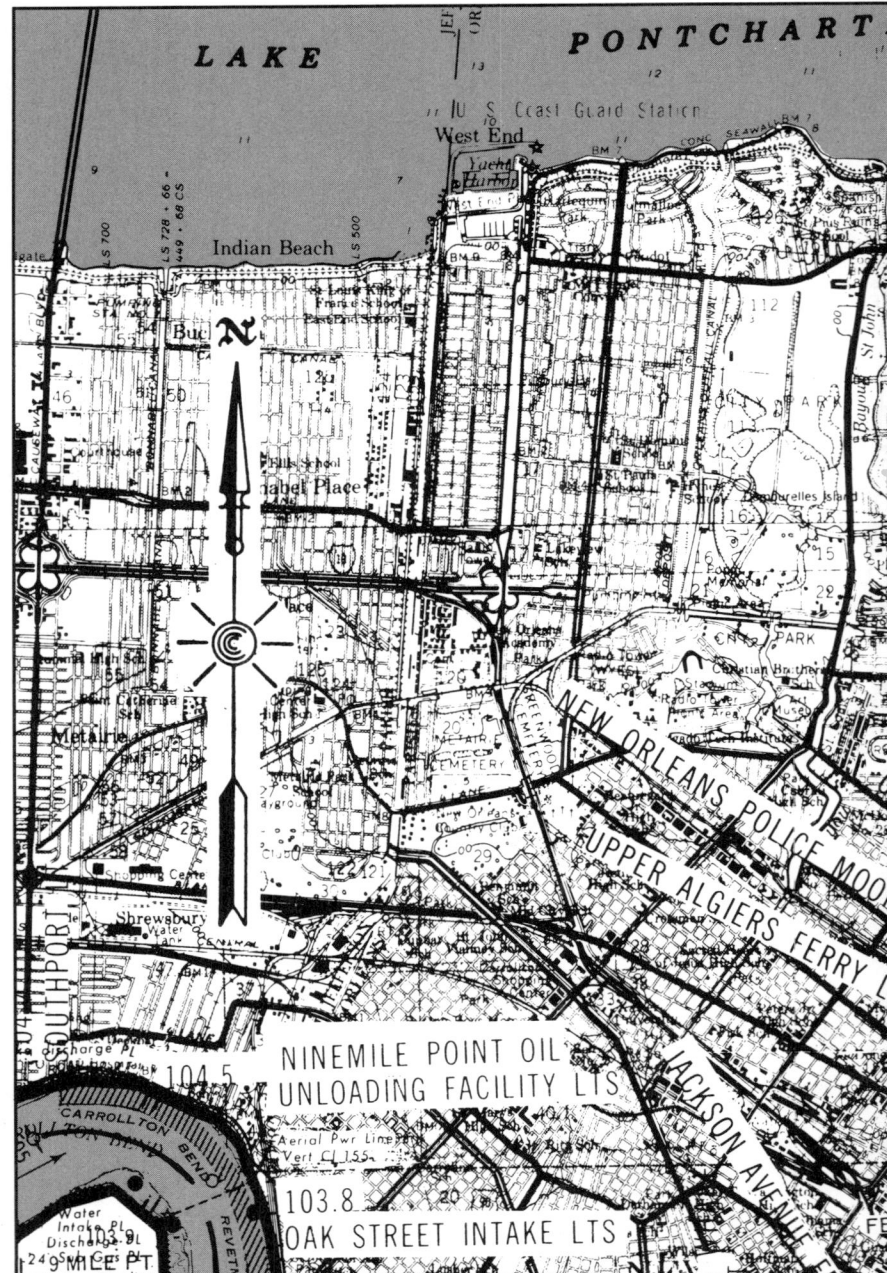

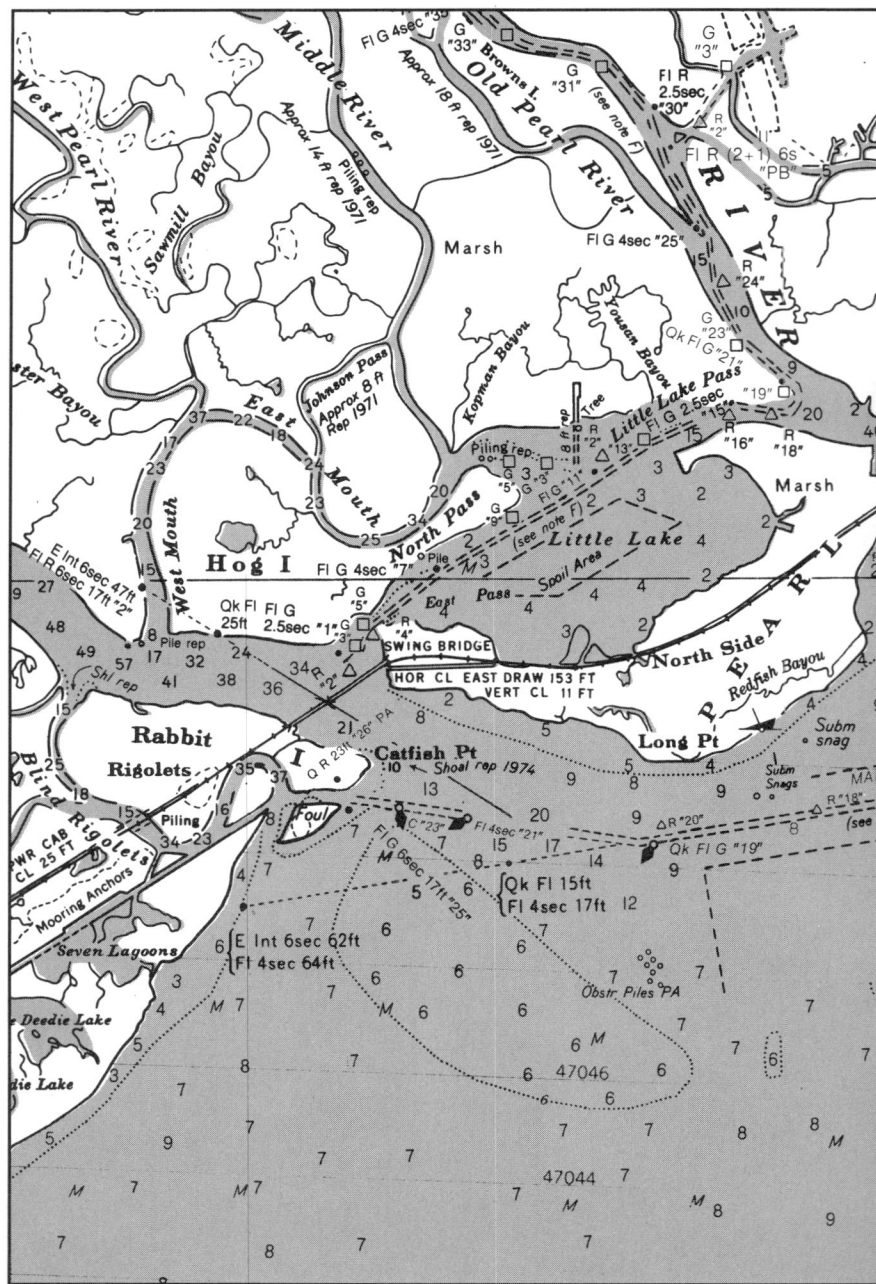

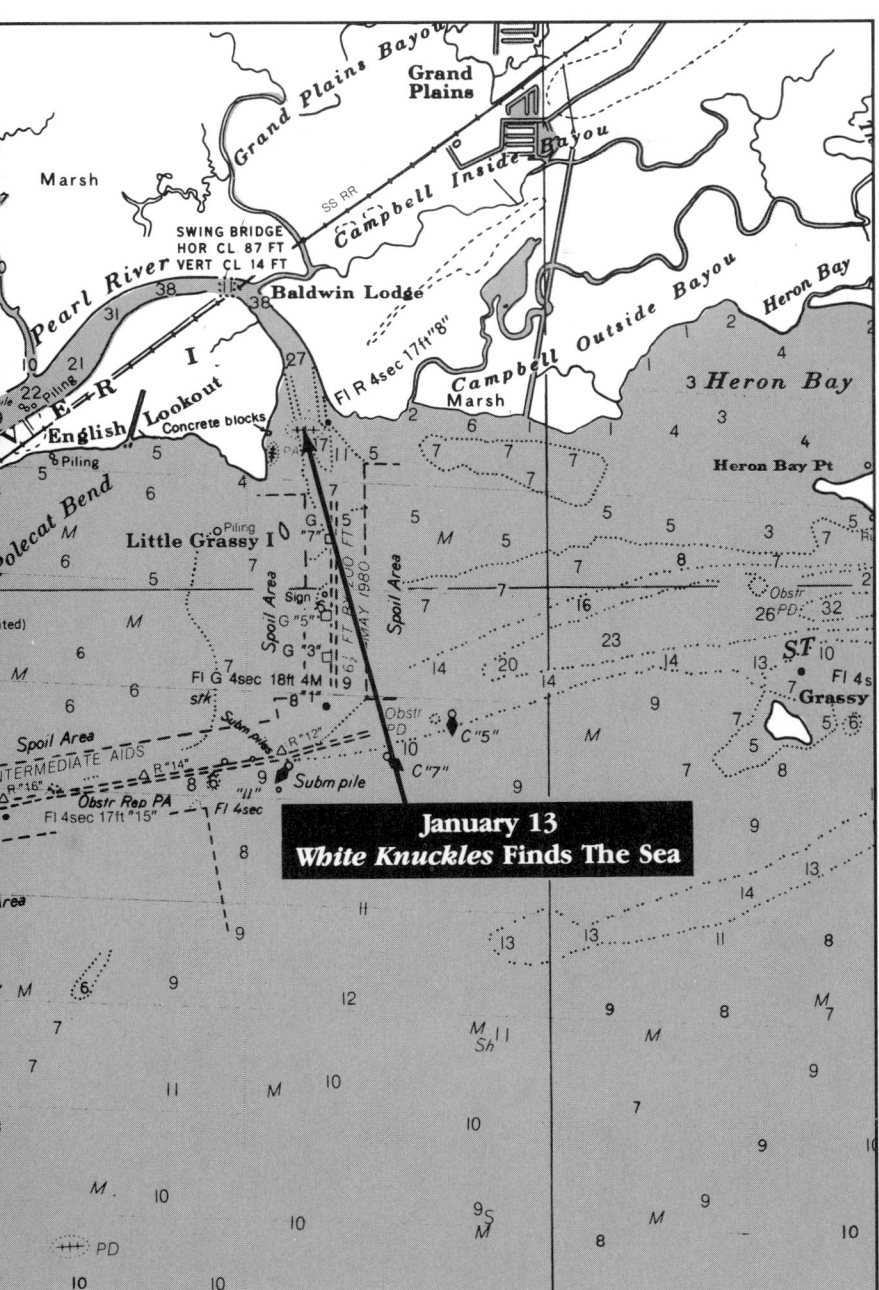

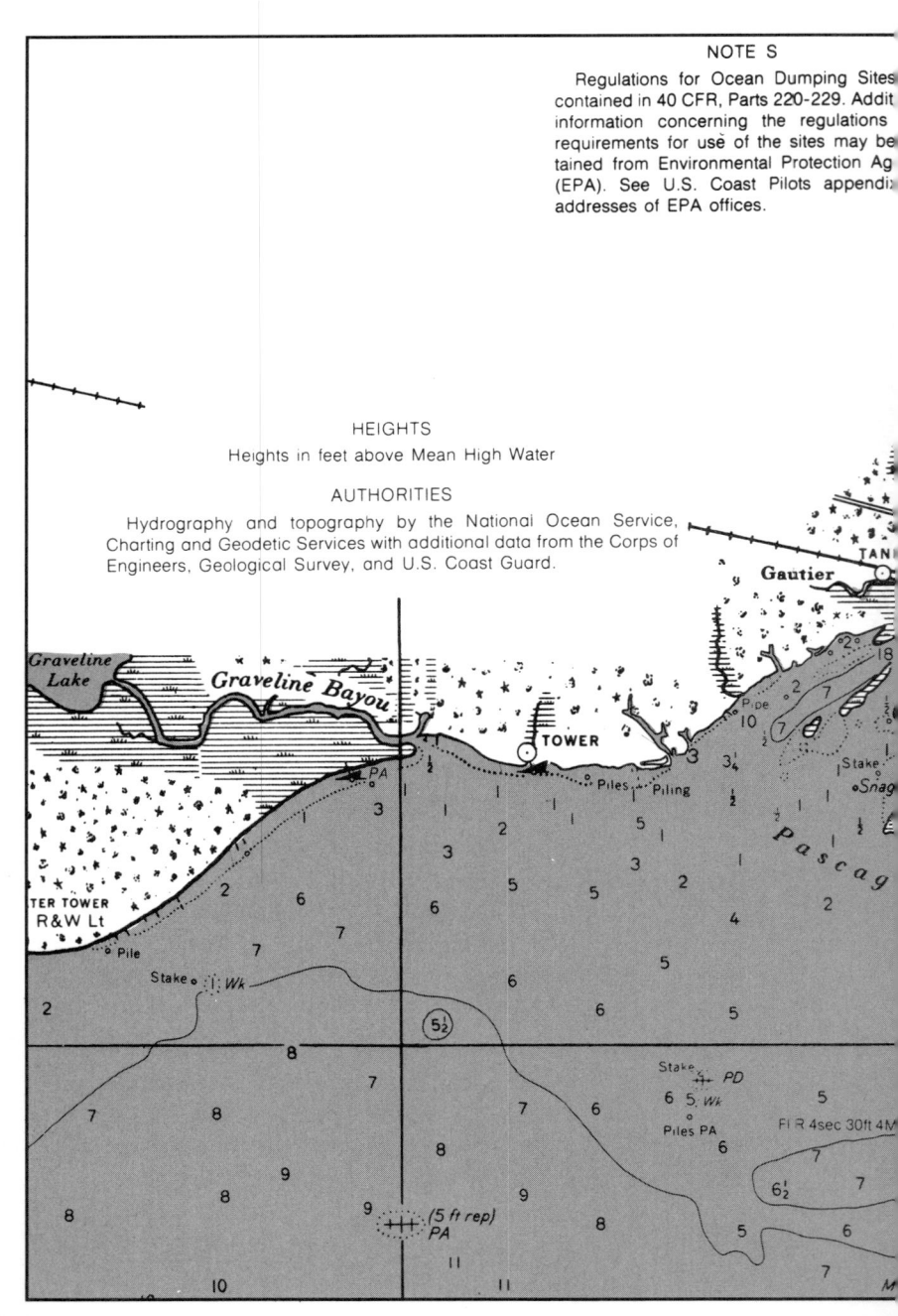

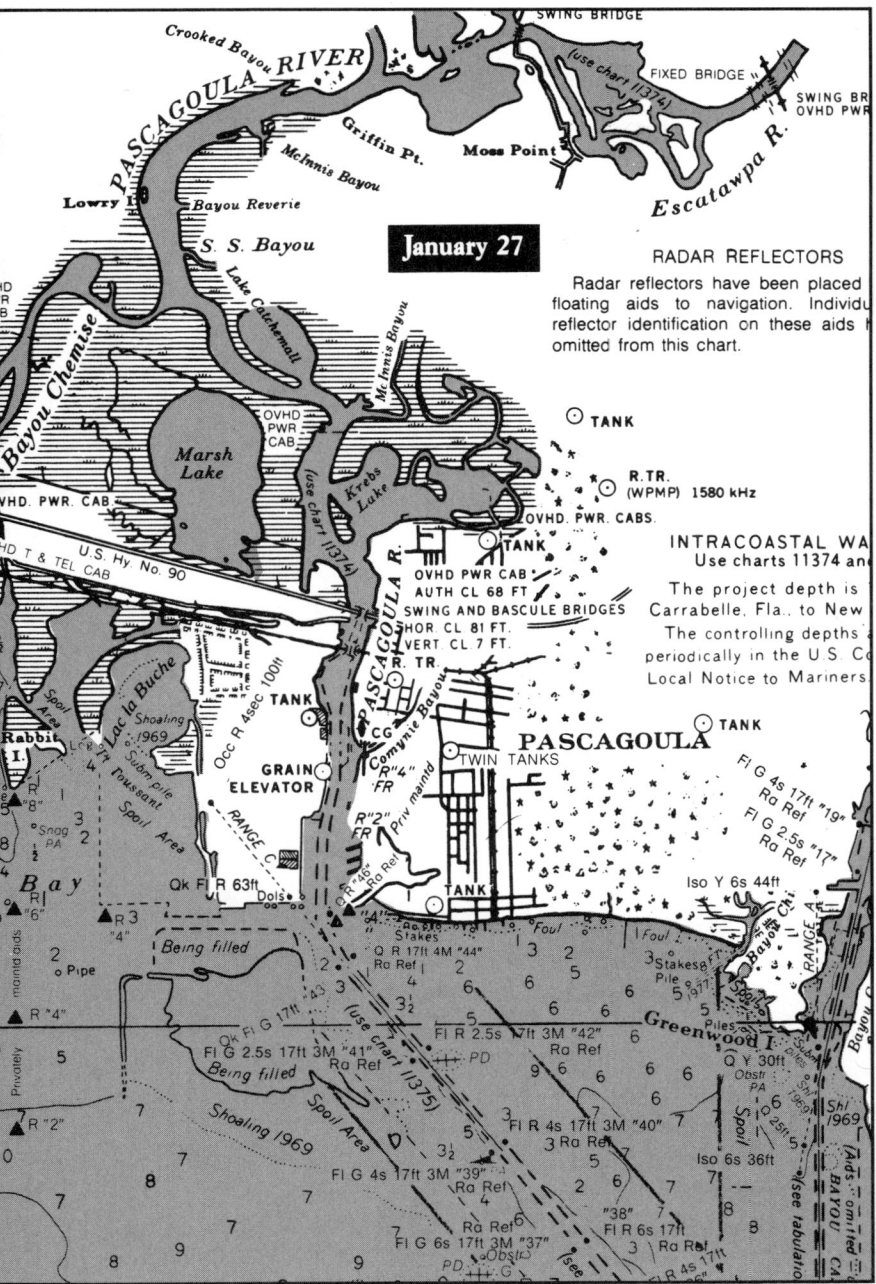

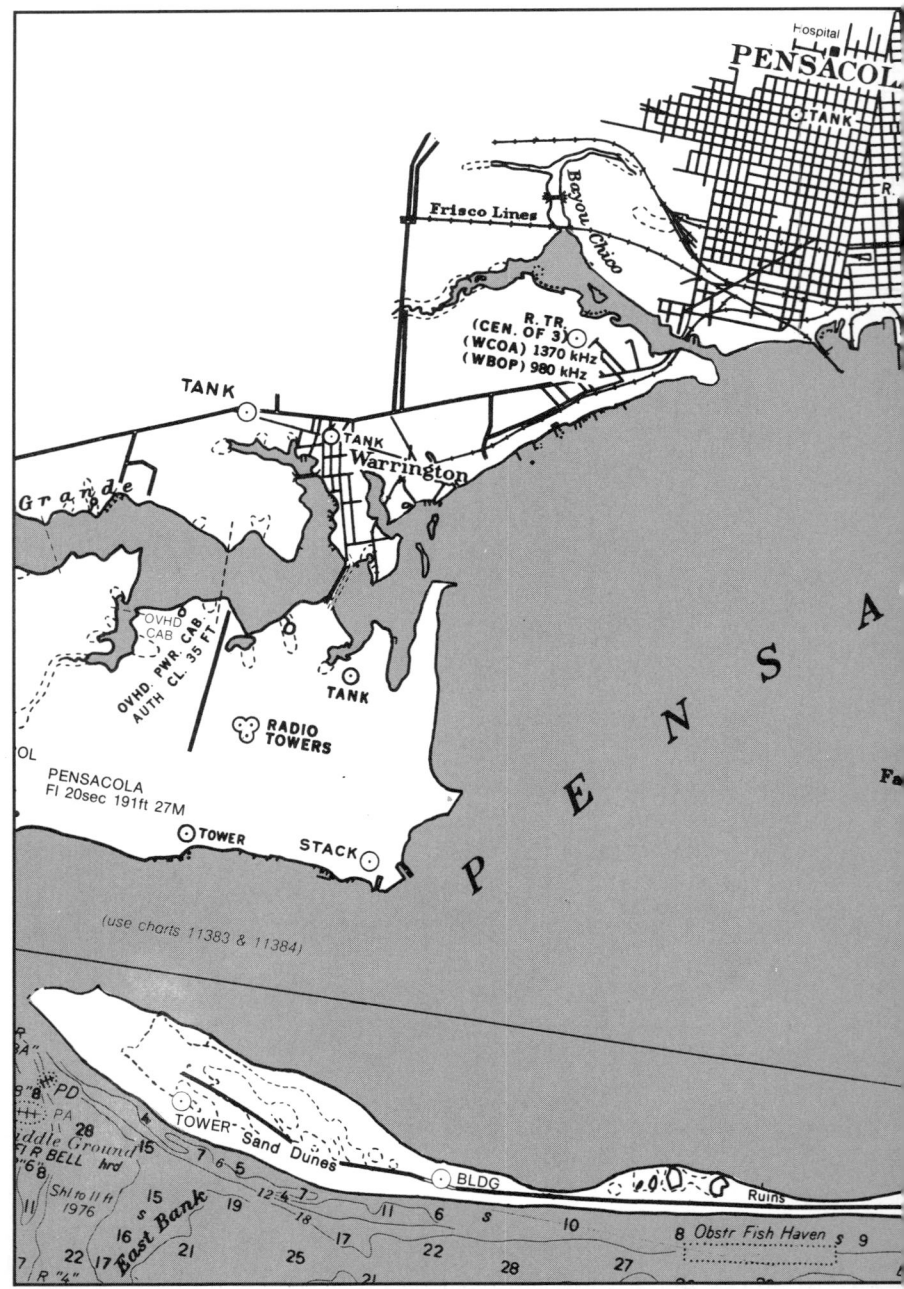

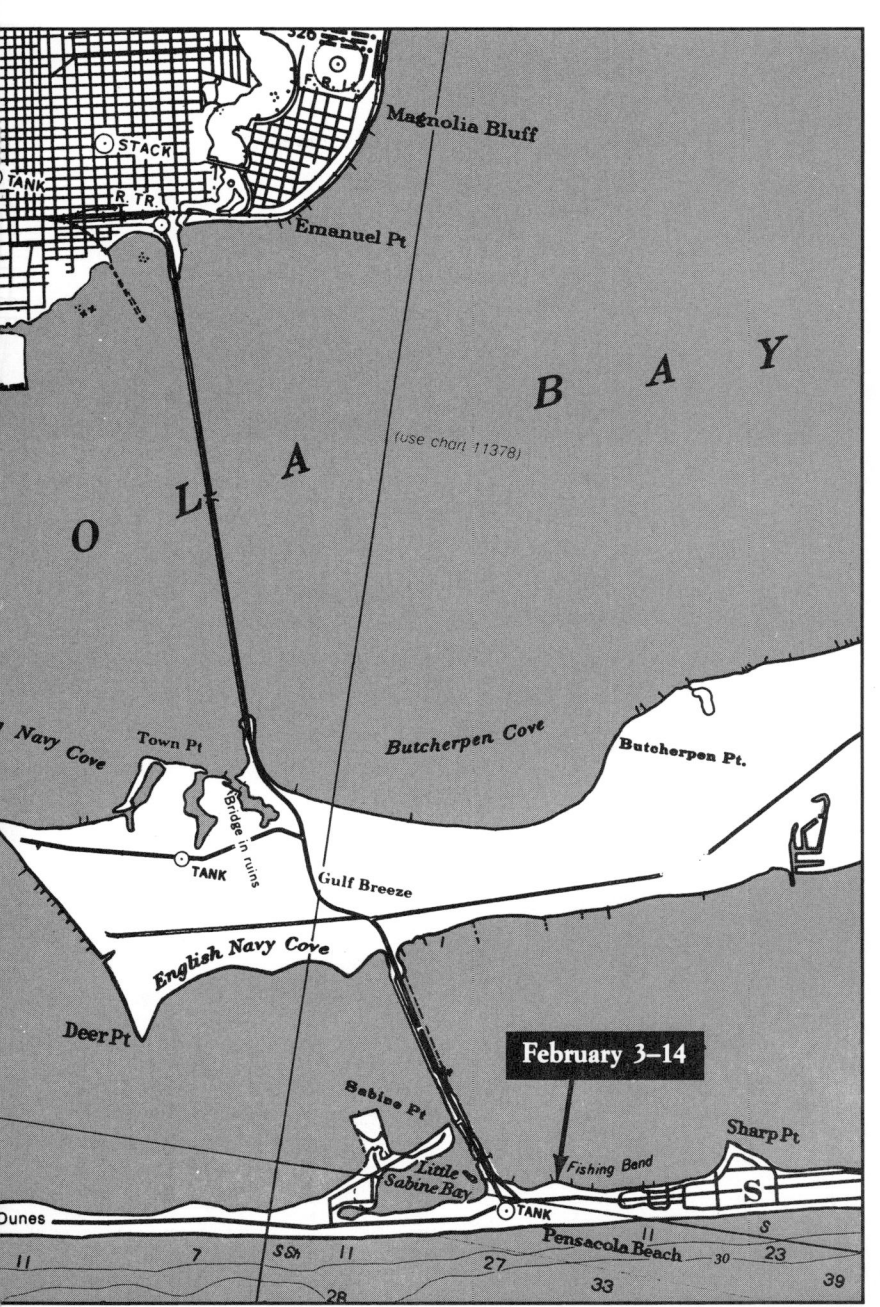

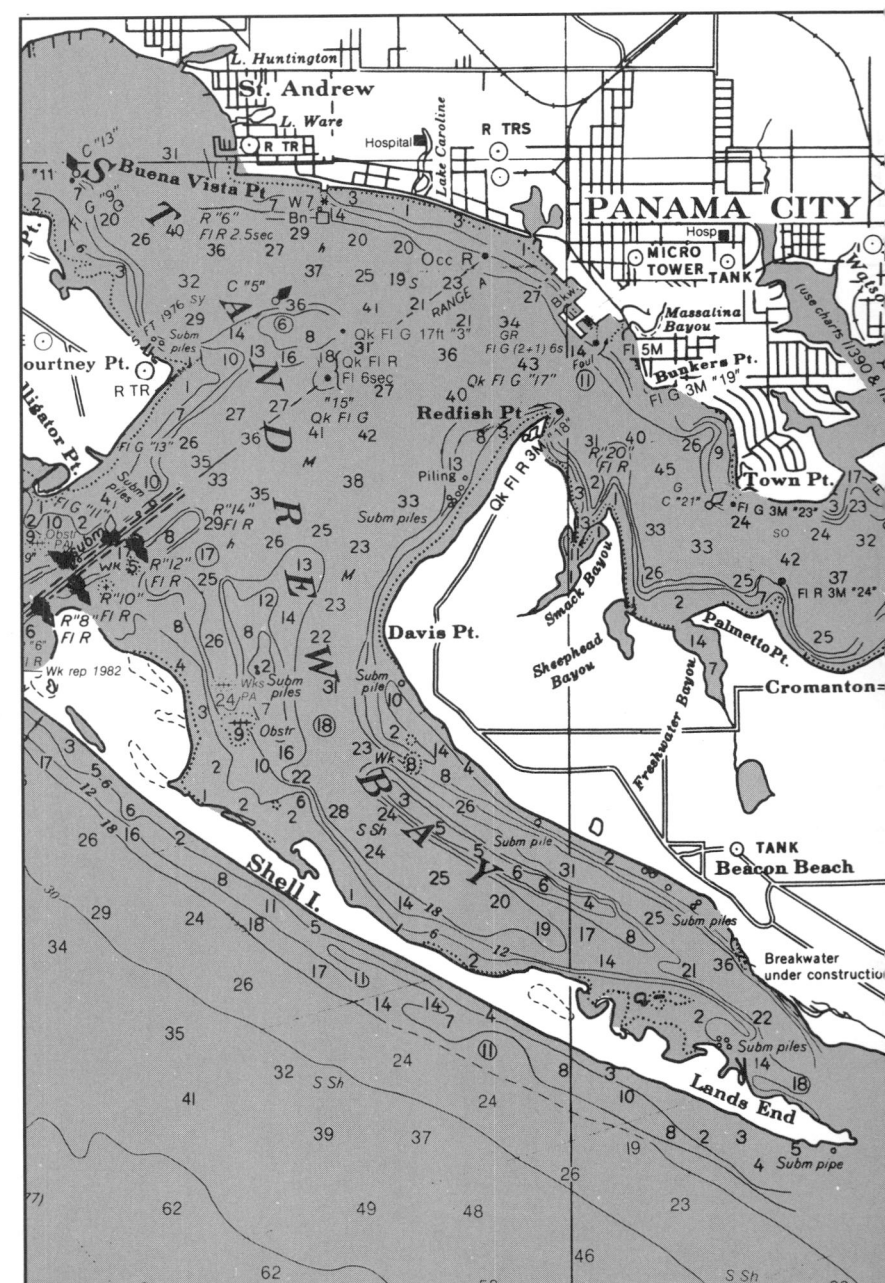

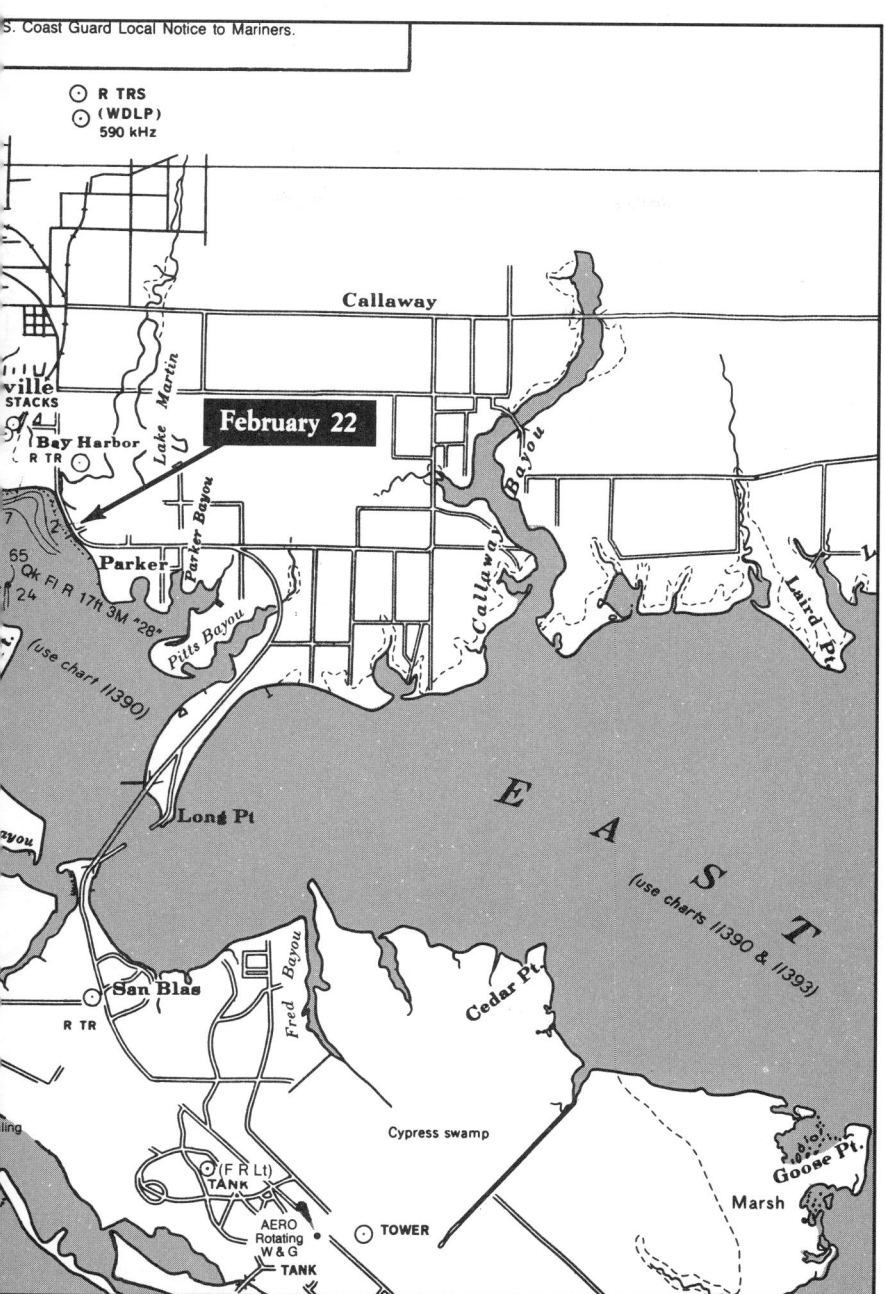

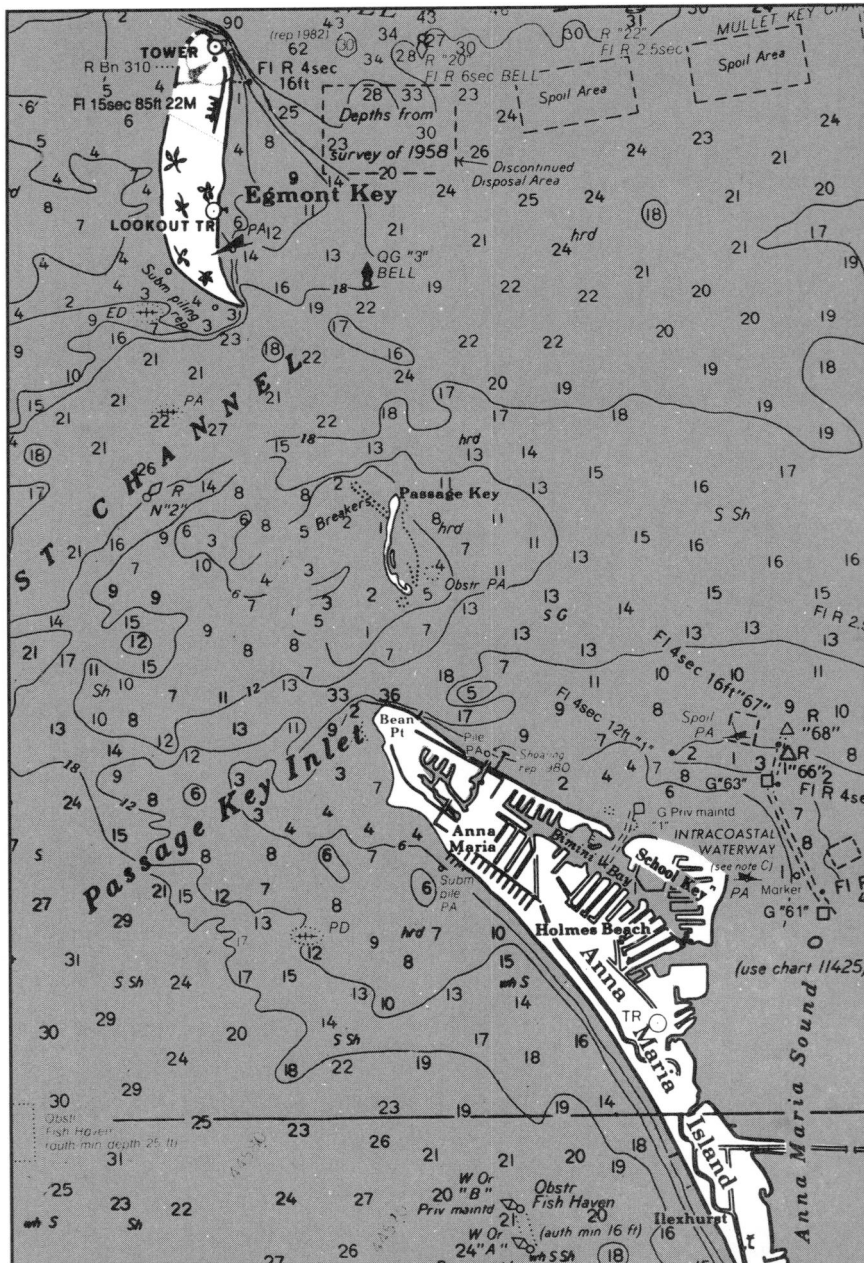

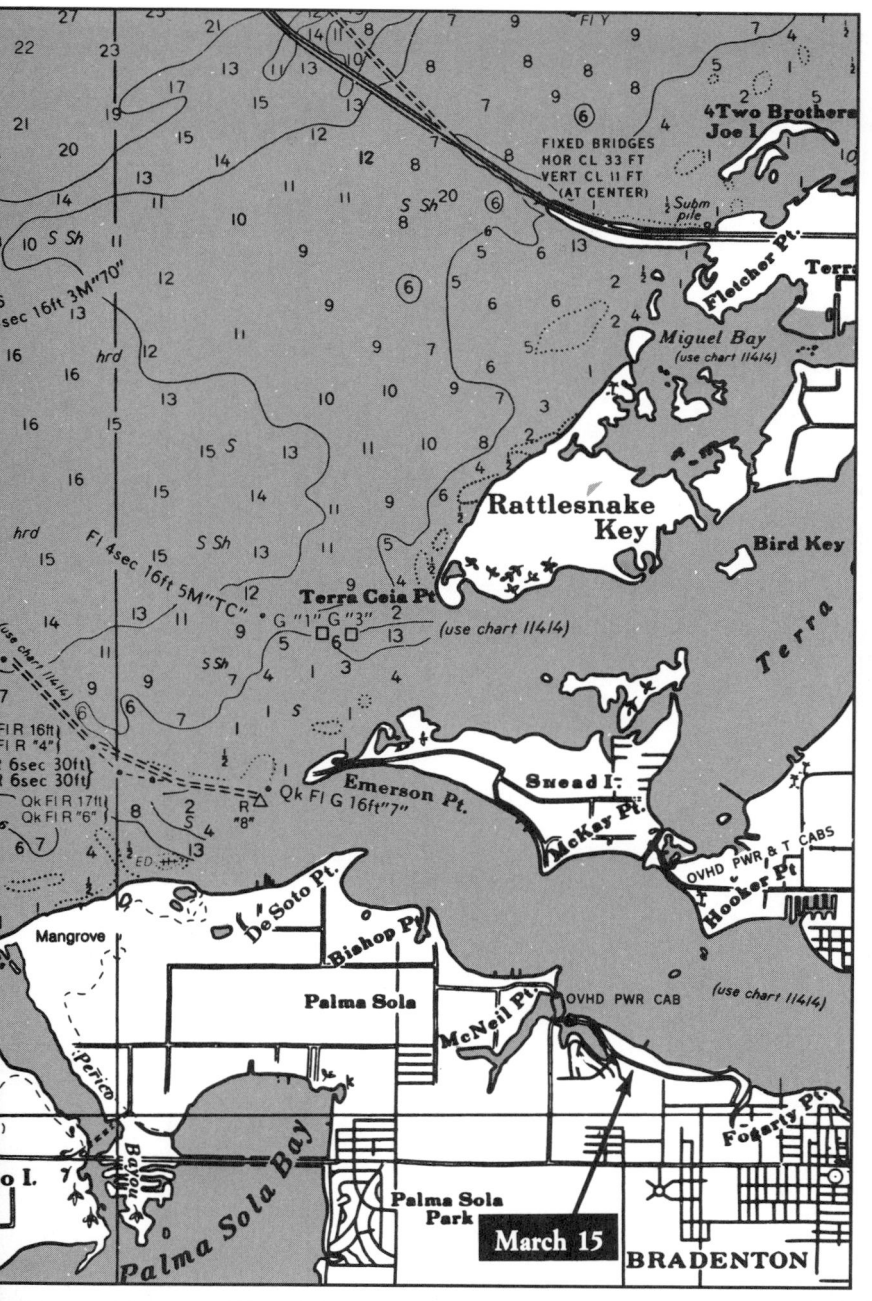

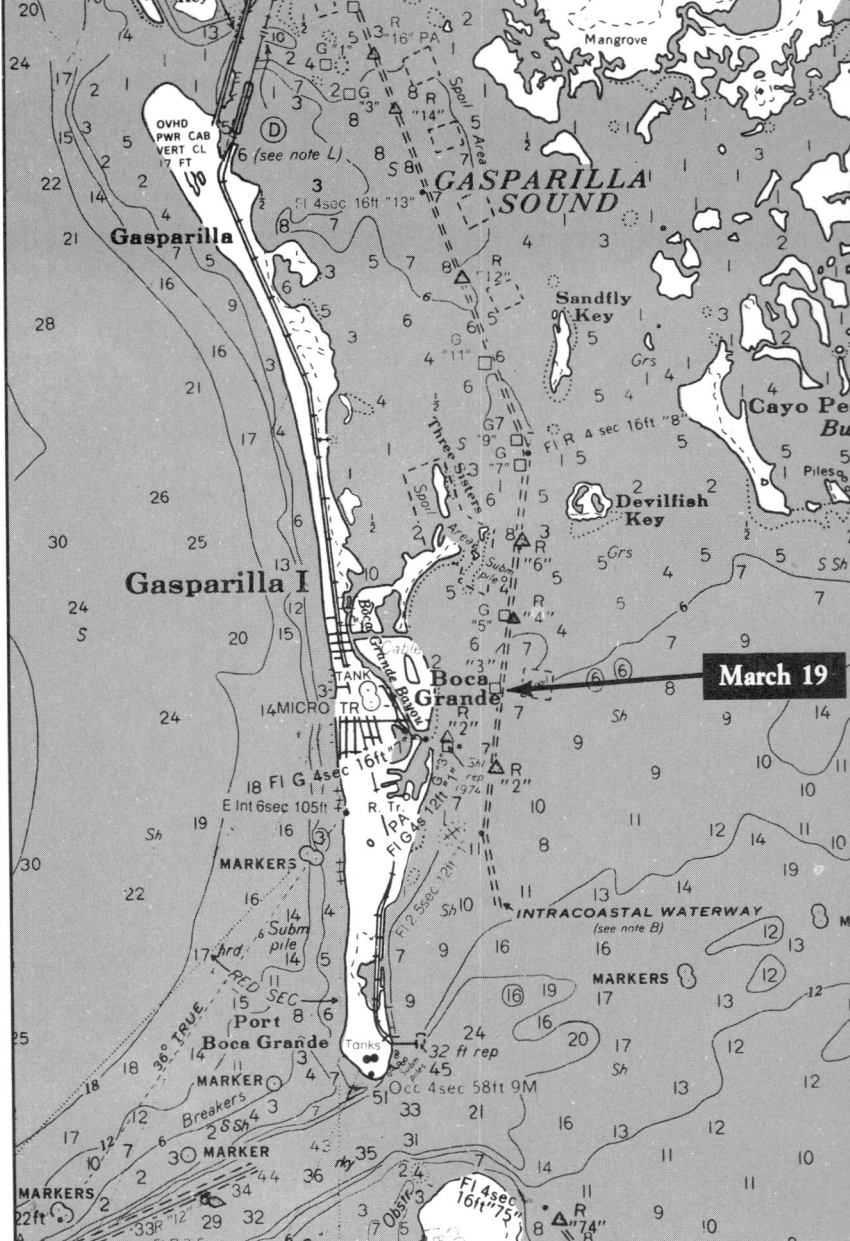

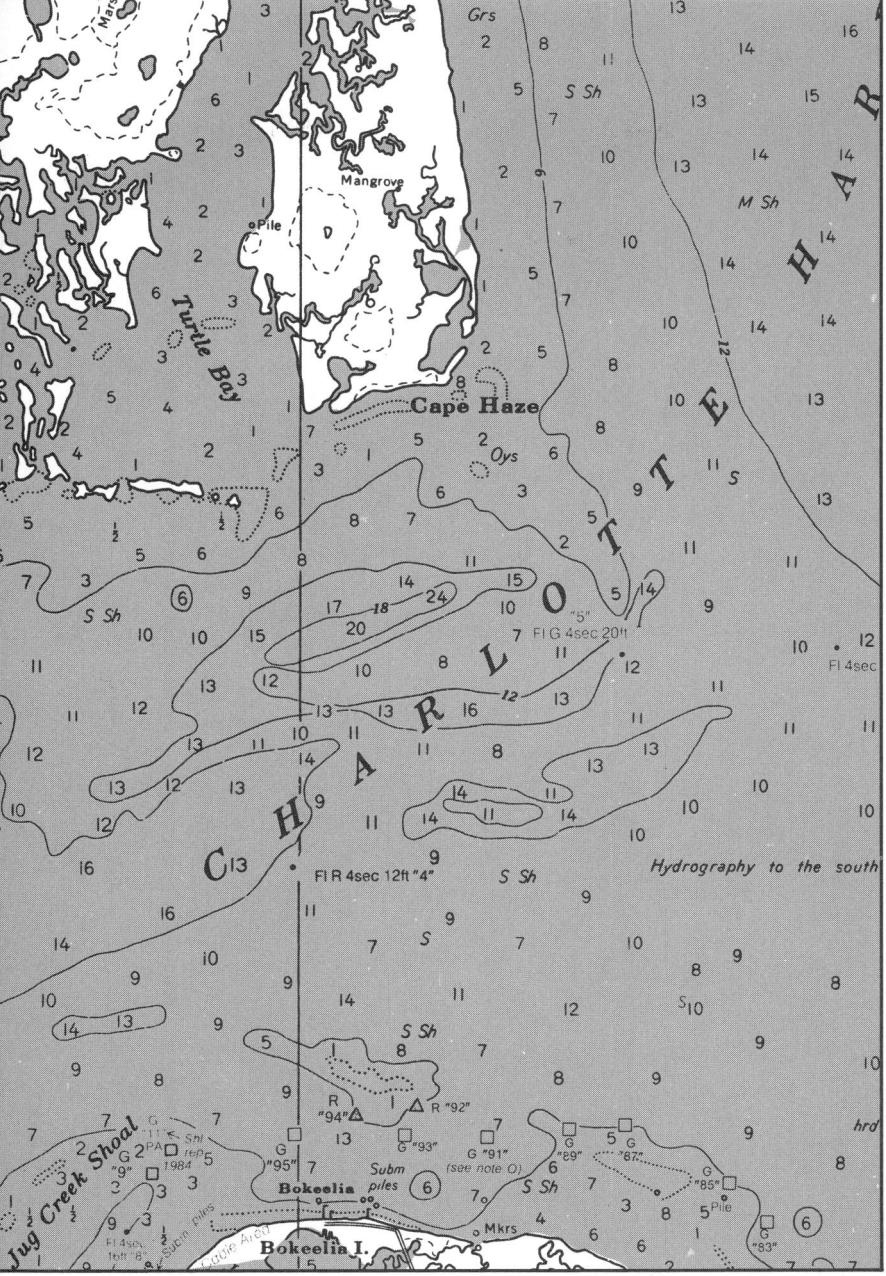

January 30
Front Point, Florida

We're still fighting that east wind, which, I'm told, always follows a north wind in these parts. We made it to a wrecked marina at Front Point, just on the outskirts of Pensacola. There are no services here, but before Hurricane Frederic there were cafés, shops, and two boat-repair places. The owner of this marina is rebuilding, but he is faced with the problem of material and labor shortages. I fear John is disappointed by our slow progress.

January 31

Last night the wind shifted to the north and was strong enough to drive most of the water out of the small bay, leaving us aground. The marina manager advised me that we'd probably remain aground as long as the wind stayed from the north — even the high tide (only one foot) could not come in against a norther.

February 1

The norther continued all day, and we remained aground — a most boring way to spend a day! John and I whiled away the hours by playing cards, checkers, and dominoes. High tide is due at 2321, and if the wind has died by then, we have hopes of floating free. If this happens, I will move the boat out to deeper water and wait for morning.

February 2
Pensacola Beach, Florida

We did not float free last night, so this morning we had to work to get out of here. I led the jib halyard over to a neighboring boat and heeled *White Knuckles* over as far as possible. I then led a line astern to a piling and began winching the boat back. After moving about four feet, she floated free, and we quickly left, bumping a few times on the way out. We had a head wind and had to beat some fourteen miles to Santa Rosa Island, where we moored at a marina in Little Sabine Bay. The owner of the marina was in the Bahama Islands. Some of the tenants suggested we use his slip, which we did, hooking up to electricity and water. Back in the lap of luxury!

February 3
Pensacola Beach, Florida

This morning, John caught a ride into Pensacola (across the bay from here) and boarded a bus for Escatawpa. I think he decided he'd enjoyed all the sailing he could stand. I told him I'd be here awhile, waiting for mail to catch up to me, in case he wanted to rejoin me. He made no comment, so I do not expect him back. I'm afraid he has classified me as his "nutty" brother.

February 4 through 14

This part of Florida, the panhandle, is the only part of the state that admits to having a winter. It gets surprisingly cold when the frequent northers sweep in. Last night, the temperature dropped to twenty-five degrees, and it barely reached fifty degrees today. Obviously, this is the off season. Most of the businesses relating to tourists — motels, restaurants, and souvenir shops — are closed. The beautiful beaches are deserted. Since I was unsuccessful in outrunning Old Man Winter, I might as well relax and move only on warm, pretty days. I'm dallying here now while I await mail from home.

I biked along the white, sugary-looking beaches today, noting the deep blue hues of the water and the just-as-blue sky. The air is cool and crisp, with a northeast wind creating seas five to seven feet. Motels had *no vacancy* signs up, but that is because they are closed for the season.

Santa Rosa Island is very beautiful and unspoiled — and rather lonesome right now. There are not too many permanent residents on the island. Most of those who live here work across the bay in Pensacola, so during the day I feel very left out and alone. On the coldest days I will no doubt get in a lot of reading. On a warm day I plan to visit Pensacola, about eight miles from here. I will move on as soon as I receive mail, but the weather probably will not improve until we get out of the northern waters of Florida, past Carabelle, some 200 miles from here. I am not equipped to sail from here directly to the Florida Keys — I have no knowledge of celestial navigation nor the instruments for it — so we must stay in the Intracoastal Waterway in its eastward reach to Carabelle. From Carabelle, we will take the Big Bend route to southern Florida. This is not a well buoyed route and is not considered part of the Intracoastal Waterway — I am a little apprehensive about it. I understand there are some buoys, but they are so far apart that it's impossible to see from one to the next. I have been advised that one should wait at Carabelle for a good norther and then scoot south with it.

· Today I biked into Pensacola and was disappointed to find that most everything had moved to the suburbs, a malady that has struck most of our cities. The shopping centers and stores I needed to visit were too far in the outskirts for me to reach on my bicycle.

Downtown Pensacola is practically dead. All that remains are some large banks (which probably made the loans for the moves to suburbia), some renovated historical buildings, the docks, and a few small shops. Once Pensacola was the home port of the world's largest red-snapper fleet, as well as many shrimp and oyster boats. Pensacola has a colorful history, having been under the flags of Spain, France, England, the Confederacy, and the United States. The first permanent settlement took place in 1698 under the name of Fort San Carlos. It was here that Governor Andrew Jackson purchased Florida from Spain in 1821.

On another day, I attempted to bike to Fort Pickens on Santa Rosa Island. However, the road was closed, and a notice on the gate indicated that the area was off limits because of drifting waves. Fort Pickens is one of the federal forts in the South that the rebels never succeeded in capturing.

The following day, *White Knuckles* acquired a baby. I purchased an eight-foot sailing dinghy. After sailing it around this small bay for several hours, I tied it to the mother ship, and it is nudging like a baby calf searching for her dinner. Coincidentally, the dink is built by a company whose name begins with an *H* so that its sail has an *H* on it, as does *White Knuckles's* mainsail. The dink is cat rigged for sailing and can also be rowed or powered with a small outboard motor. I chose to take the two oars, but I had no desire to own another motor.

February 15

This morning we slipped our mooring lines and set sail for Fort Walton Beach, but traveled only a few miles. Off to starboard, I saw the prettiest little cove with the whitest beach, a few trees, and no houses. It was a beautiful sunny day, and I could not resist this little cove. I promptly dropped sails and anchor, hoisted sail on the dink, went ashore, and walked the beach looking for shells and flotsam. I rested in the shade of a tree and almost fell asleep. Upon returning to the boat, I tuned in to the weather report and learned that I should not have tarried here. The weather is supposed to get worse during the night, becoming colder and windy. We are protected here from east, south, and west winds, but if the predicted norther comes in, it may get very uncomfortable riding at anchor here because we are exposed to the north and sitting in shallow water. I'm hoping the norther doesn't arrive until morning so that we can shoot through the narrows just east of here and get on to Fort Walton Beach. The narrows are just what the name implies, and they cover about ten miles. One needs a north or south wind to sail through this narrow stretch of the waterway. I'm told that east and west winds make the waterway very choppy and rough. There is a good tidal current through it, running east or west, depending on the time of day. We may pay a price for stopping here, but I'm still glad we did.

February 16

The norther I spoke of was predicted to arrive in midafternoon, so we sailed out of our pretty little cove at about 0900, hoping to be in Fort Walton Beach by the time the norther arrived there. We were just approaching the narrows at noon when the norther struck viciously and without warning. I doused the jib sail since the wind and rain kept increasing. The mainsail needed a reef taken in it; by then we were on a sleigh ride, the fastest I've ever experienced. I dared not leave the tiller to reef the main. We were now in a very narrow channel, with breakers to our immediate starboard and sandy bottom to port. The strong wind had pushed the waters southward. I was towing the dink, and it was in danger of becoming swamped. We zipped under a bridge. Then I saw a cove to port that looked promising. I headed up and worked my way back and forth into it as far as I dared. I dropped anchor, hoping the wind had already pushed out all the water it was going to. After making all secure, I retired to the cabin.

By this time I was very cold and wet. The temperature had dropped from seventy degrees to forty degrees in less than an hour. These frequent Florida northers are just as bad as the ones we have in Oklahoma. After getting into dry clothes and having some coffee, I examined the chart more carefully and read the fine print that described this cove, "Restricted — see note A on chart #1." I do not possess chart #1, and therefore have no idea what the restriction is. I hope it is restricted to sailboats, twenty-five feet and under. In any event, I have no choice but to remain here until the wind and seas subside. I do not want to lose the dink on her maiden voyage.

Before purchasing this dink, I measured the foredeck on *White Knuckles* and saw that I could carry an eight-foot dink and still have room to work the sails. However, I did not take into account the beams of the boat and dink; I discovered too late that I cannot carry it there — so I towed it. It has a skeg and is easy to tow under normal conditions. But today's high winds and rough seas were almost too much for the little gal. I feared that if it wallowed about long enough and filled with water, the painter on the bow eye would break, and the dink would be lost. Later, I intend to invert the dink over the cabin top, but I am afraid it will take up too much room there. I have never read of anything but bad experiences when it comes to towing dinks. I simply must find a place to carry this one as soon as *White Knuckles* and I leave the Intracoastal Waterway at Carabelle.

February 17
Fort Walton Beach, Florida

This noon the wind abated somewhat, getting ready to shift to the east. We left our anchorage at about 1300 under reefed main only. It was a thrilling, though somewhat anxious, sail. The narrows weave around several small islands, and we dodged back and forth to avoid shoal water. The dink was well ballasted by incoming water and towed nicely. I had attached an extra painter, leaving it a little slack, so that if the first one broke, the extra one could take over the towing. We arrived at Fort Walton Beach at 1430 just before the wind came east, so we did have to beat upwind. We will remain here, doing laundry and shopping, until the wind shifts to the south, which it usually does after swinging from north to east.

February 18

Today I rode my bike to Mary Esther, a small town adjoining Fort Walton Beach. Mary Esther has a huge shopping mall, where I was able to obtain supplies. The name of the town appealed to me, which is why I decided to go the few miles and see it for myself. Mary Esther is a village of well-to-do citizens with beachfront homes and boat docks — all very nice, well groomed, and quiet. People told me it is not so quiet when the tourists arrive, and although many of them rely on tourism for their livlihoods, they didn't seem too anxious for the busy season to arrive.

I returned home to the boat about midafternoon and spent the rest of the day playing with the dinghy. With stick-on lettering, I named her *White Knuckles* after her mother.

February 19

Today, I visited a trihull, forty-eight feet in length, aboard which a family lives full time. The boat had been seized with a load of dope by the Coast Guard. Later it was auctioned off, and the present owner was the high bidder. This is the second such boat I have seen since leaving New Orleans. The first was a sailboat from Houston, Texas, that had been seized in Pensacola.

February 20
Joe's Bayou, near Destin, Florida

Today we moved on, only about ten miles, to our "jumping-off place," from which we plan to cross Choctawhatchee Bay. This is the last good anchoring spot this side of the large bay. From here it will be necessary to steer by compass (eighty-seven-and-a-half degrees) because the banks are not within sight of each other. I wanted to start across this bay from as near to the first bank as possible. There is a marina in this quiet little bayou, but I chose to anchor nearby. The cost of berths is steadily increasing the farther we go. On the Mississippi it was ten cents per foot of boat length, in New Orleans it was twenty cents, at Pensacola it was thirty cents, and at Fort Walton Beach it was thirty-five cents. I will try to stock up more completely and do more anchoring from here on.

There is a lot of barge traffic in this area, but this is not nearly the problem it was on the Mississippi. I've seen only one, two, or occasionally three barges per tow, and they must be under a speed limit because they move very slowly.

February 21
Choctawhatchee Bay, Florida

We sailed out of Joe's Bayou in a thick fog this morning. I could see nothing but the compass, but since I had to steer by compass regardless of the weather, we scampered on across Choctawhatchee Bay with a good south wind on our starboard. At the eastern end of the bay, the waterway enters "the ditch," a long, narrow canal leading to Saint Andrew's Bay. We must try to run it in a day, as it is too narrow to moor or anchor in. We anchored just before entering the ditch and will try to start on it tomorrow. It was fifteen degrees today, and tonight thunderstorms are building. I'm hoping the weather will clear by morning.

February 22
Panama City, Florida

To my complete surprise, we docked in Panama City at 1500 (I had thought it too far for one day's sail). We got an early start and ran the ditch on motor power only. As soon as we cleared the lift bridge and entered West Bay of Saint Andrew's Bay, I hoisted sail. Thunderstorms were building, and we had strong, variable winds. The bay was rough, but we plowed on through the west part of it in short order and got moored just minutes before the rains came. The marina here is just before the second bridge, and within two blocks I found a motel, laundry, grocery store, and many other businesses. This would be a nice, handy place to spend some time, but I would like to move on tomorrow — weather permitting — toward Carabelle. I believe Carabelle is seventy miles from here, and two days should do it.

My days are short ones — I like to start late and stop early. I find myself too weary whenever I spend a long day in the cockpit, especially when a lot of beating, tacking, and sail changing is involved. I love it, but I lack the stamina that I had a few years ago.

Saint Andrew's Bay is a very good refuge for ships when hurricanes threaten. The bay is practically landlocked and offers much protected water. However, small boats should seek other shelter; the bay is large and shallow and makes rough anchorage for a small boat in heavy weather.

The ditch we traversed this morning was unlike any canal we have seen before. The banks were twenty-five to fifty feet high, topped with tall pine trees. I could see none of the countryside; we seemed to be passing through a green tunnel. It was lonely; we met only one boat through the entire length of the canal.

February 25
Overstreet, Florida

We left Panama City at 1100 today. Heavy winds from the north forced us to sail under reefed main only. The forecast called for northerly winds shifting to northwest later in the day, an ideal situation as we headed east. We ran and reached the remainder of West Bay and all of East Bay. Then we entered another canal that runs inland through swamps, past Overstreet, White City, and on to Apalachicola Bay. The chart describes the swamps as *Panther Swamp, Cypress Swamp,* and *Low Lying Swamp.* One area is captioned *Impenetrable Swamp.* The canal is lined with pine trees, so one cannot see much of the swamps. Until today, I had seen many birds — egrets, I think — sitting on the buoys. Bird deposits make it difficult to distinguish the colors of the buoys. Today I began to see a lot of pelicans sitting on the buoys also. They are not in the least frightened of boats. They just sit and stare, slowly turning their heads as they watch the boat pass by. The egrets usually take wing when the boat gets close to their perch. As we crossed East Bay, a few dolphins played along with us. They would be at the bow awhile, then surface at the stern, blow, and race back to the bow. Once I thought one hit the dinghy, but I was not sure. The dolphins seem to be curious about *White Knuckles* and act happy and mischievous. They are lovable creatures.

The bridge here at Overstreet is a pontoon, the first structure of this kind that we have encountered. It consists of a barge that swings out of the way for boat traffic. I meant to stop for the night just above the bridge, but it swung open for me as I drew close. I came on past it and anchored right against the bank, which is overgrown with tall swamp grass.

February 26

We unintentionally spent another day here. I was all ready for an early morning departure but could not raise the anchor. The tide had dropped, and I could not get the boat directly over the anchor because of a mud bank. About noon I tried again, to no avail. High tide was 1700, and I got the boat over the anchor but was unable to budge it. Feeling around with the boat hooks, I discovered that the anchor was hung in some wreckage or something metallic. A kind gentleman living nearby noticed my dilemma, and he offered to pull the anchor out with his tractor. I dropped a line down the anchor chain with a slipknot on it and led the other end ashore to the tractor. I then got back on the boat to feed out the anchor rope as the tractor hauled away. Suddenly the tractor stopped, and we discovered that the anchor was now buried deeply in the bank. The boat was free, but the tractor was anchored firmly. We had to dig the anchor out with a shovel. By this time it was dark. I moved the boat to a higher bank, threw the anchor up in the sawgrass, and called it a day.

February 27
Apalachicola, Florida

At 0700 this morning I stepped ashore from the bow pulpit, retrieved the anchor from the grass, and departed from Overstreet. I felt we had spent enough time there. The canal was narrow and twisting, so we cruised under mainsail and motor. Soon the canal led us into Lake Wimico where I killed the motor and hoisted the lapper. We sailed the five miles across this lake. Then we re-entered the canal and before long reached the Apalachicola River. About two miles of this river put us in downtown Apalachicola. We stopped at a very nice marina motel just above the Highway 98 bridge. We will spend about a week here waiting for mail, doing laundry, shopping, and resting.

February 28 through March 9

Today we moved from the marina, which was costing seven-and-a-half dollars per day, past the highway bridge to the municipal yacht harbor, which costs fifteen dollars per month, including electricity and water. This yacht harbor is hard against a nice city park, and by street we are only two blocks from where we were yesterday. No commercial boats are permitted here. At present the harbor is occupied by four sailboats, two houseboats, and one cruiser. I am the only owner present; the others have left their boats here for one reason or another. The police (who collect the dock fees) told me of a thirty-eight-foot sailboat that came here during the night about two months ago. Although the boat still sits here, they have never seen the owner and do not known his name or where he is.

Apalachicola is mainly a fishing port. There must be a hundred shrimp boats here and even more oyster boats. The shrimp boats do not seem to be doing much at this time, but the oyster boats are very busy. This is the oyster capital of Florida, but the oystermen are in hard times at present. The government has declared oysters from this area to be unsafe for human consumption because of polluted waters. The oystermen think the situation will be cleared up shortly and that the government is mistaken — which in my opinion is very likely.

Apalachicola was the home of Dr. John Gorrie, who invented the method of manufacturing ice. His work, which led to his discovery, is on exhibit in a small museum located here.

I talked with a shrimp boat captain today, and during our conversation he asked me why I never lock my boat when leaving it to run errands or wander about. I replied that one had to trust his fellow man at times and that I would find no enjoyment in my sightseeing if I had to constantly worry about theft. He heartily agreed with me and said that the surest way to get one's boat broken into would be to act snobbish, distrustful, and fearful for one's gadgets and equipment. He also said that many fancy sailors stopped here who glared about at other people as if their boats were loaded with gold. These local people are honest and hardworking, and they would not touch another man's boat without his knowledge or consent. They watch over a visitor's boat, keeping an eye on his mooring lines and bumpers.

I have not locked my boat since leaving New Orleans and have been away from it many times for up to a full day. I have had no unwelcome visitors. Had I locked it, I would not have been able to keep it as dry and sweet-smelling as it is. I leave it open at every opportunity and go on about my errands or whatever.

My main problem at this point is that I don't know when I can move on. March is a bad time of the year in this area, and the weather does not improve until May. One front after another has been moving through, with no more than twenty-four hours between them. If we follow the Big Bend route, which stays close to shore, we will be in shallow water with a possible lee shore. Going directly toward Tampa Bay involves over fifty hours of running time, which could get us caught in one of these storms — but at least the water is deeper. The locals advise me to go no further alone. However, tomorrow, March 10, I will make a firm decision and leave here. I'll either go to Carabelle and cross from there or head directly toward Tampa Bay. I have the necessary charts for either route, a good compass, and plenty of provisions. I am short on knowledge and nerve, and I have no electronic aids at all.

March 10

I have been in daily contact, by telephone, with the weather bureau. They will advise me when I can expect two days of good weather. So far, day after day, conditions have not been favorable for a direct crossing to Tampa Bay, and that is the route I have decided on.

March 12

Today the weather boys finally said that the next four days should be favorable. However, they advised me to wait twenty-four hours for the heavy seas to calm down. Afraid that another front will sneak in by then, I have decided to leave come morning, which means beginning a journey on the 13th. Fortunately, I'm not all that superstitious.

March 15
Bradenton, Florida

We made the crossing to Tampa Bay in about forty-eight hours, then continued on to Bradenton — actually the village of Cortez — before berthing. I had been without sleep for fifty-two hours. The crossing was not without incident, but was a fast one as we were blessed with following seas and wind. Upon reaching the marina, I tied up at the first dock we came to, planning to go to the office, register, and be assigned a dock. First I just wanted to lie down for a few minutes.

Some four hours later I awoke. I did not know where I was. I was more completely disoriented than ever before in my life. I staggered around the dock, ashamed to ask anyone where I was. Finally I consulted my chart and saw where I had checked off the entrance buoy to Tampa Bay. I then presented myself to the marina office, signed in, moved to a permanent dock, then went back to sleep for six more hours, awakening rested but very hungry.

What a crossing it was! The seas were very heavy, as predicted, and this caused serious problems with the dink I was towing. It would surf down a huge wave and crash mightily into the stern of the boat. This was battering the bow and the bow eye of the dink badly. I knew it would never withstand such treatment for two days. I tried pulling the dink up alongside the big boat, but this threatened to swamp it. I had two tow lines attached to it — one from the bow eye and one wrapped completely around it at the gunwales. The bow eye finally gave out, and when the other line pulled taut, the dink turned around, and I wound up towing it in reverse. After working the dink up alongside again and half hoisting it aboard, I managed to repair the bow eye. By then the seas had calmed somewhat, and my problems seemed to be over. We were under full sail, and I had been fighting the tiller throughout this ordeal. This episode with the dinghy lasted about four hours and almost exhausted me.

As it turned out, my problems were far from over. During the first night, the bike tore loose from its lashings and hung on the lifeline by the handlebars, banging the boat terribly. I almost tossed it overboard. Finally I managed to get it up on the cabin top and lashed it securely. The weather boys had said the seas would be ten to twelve feet, but in my humble opinion they were twelve to fifteen feet. They did not seem so bad at night because I could not see very much, but the sound of breaking waves coming up from astern was unnerving. *White Knuckles,* however, was in her element. Gallantly she plowed right on, throwing phosphorus for what seemed like twenty feet.

I admit to being terrified by what to some would be an ordinary passage. I had heard too many bad things about the gulf — its sudden weather changes and its vicious seas. A man-and-wife cruising team here told me they would never go out in the gulf alone. I replied that I would never do so again and would advise that no one do so in any boat — large or small.

MARCH 17
Sarasota, Florida

After two days of resting and licking my wounds, we left Cortez and sailed only as far as Sarasota, where I dropped anchor offshore for more rest. I was simply not up to working the boat. My arms, legs, and hands were still a mass of bruises and strained muscles. Sarasota Bay was very rough because of opposing winds and tide. We worked our way into a small cove in about ten feet of water and spent the night.

MARCH 18
Venice, Florida

I felt better today and was not quite so sore. We sailed on to Venice and spent the night at anchor. The route today led through beautiful, clear water — I could see the bottom most of the time. There were expensive and beautiful homes on each side of the waterway, many with two-boat garages. There were many palm trees along the route, beautiful green grass, and pelicans sitting on every dock and piling.

MARCH 19
Boca Grande, Florida

Today we sailed into a marina to replenish water and food supplies. Boca Grande is a very small village on the island of Gasparilla. There is one main street, one store, and one service station, but no bank.

March 20
At anchor near Fort Myers, Florida

We were some four miles from Fort Myers when darkness overtook us. I don't like going into a strange harbor at night unless it is absolutely necessary. I tacked out of the shipping channel, and when the water depth came down to seven feet, I dropped the hook for the night.

As I write today's entry, I realize that it may be my last for a while. Fort Myers presents the opportunity for restocking *White Knuckles* and, to tell the truth, my own mental and physical warehouses as well. After all, there is still so much to discover here in southern Florida.

It's been a long trip, filled with images I will never forget — the first lock *White Knuckles* and I navigated, both of us green and skittish as could be; our first day and night on the Mississippi; Vicksburg, Natchez — these memories run through me like random clips of some epic film. I won't forget the people I've met and the experiences I've had. But just as unforgettable are the faces of my wife and my children — and I know tonight, for the first time on this long journey, that soon it may be time to go home.

I've had thoughts of going home at other points on this journey, but tonight it is different. I do not think of returning home because I doubt my capabilities or because I am discouraged. Tonight's longing for home comes from a sense of completion. I have lived out my dream — *White Knuckles* and I have found the sea and sailed it.

EPILOGUE

Don McAlpine was destined to drop his anchor many more times during the spring and summer of 1980. His log entries end here, perhaps because he was ready to lay down his pen and devote his energies to exploring the islands and bays along the Florida coast. Or maybe he felt that the heart of his story — the fulfillment of a dream — had already been recorded and was available to those who would follow his example.

McAlpine sold *White Knuckles* and went home to Oklahoma City in August 1980. Soon he got the wanderlust again, bought a new sailboat, and on January 7, 1981, set out overland for Houston. There he launched the new boat and spent the next few months sailing the Gulf of Mexico along the Texas and Louisiana coasts, preparing for a trip around the world. On April 16, 1981, he went aground against a small island off the Galveston coast. As he tried to push his boat off the sand, he was caught by the wake of a barge and drowned.